OUTLAW TALES
of Idaho

OUTLAW TALES
of Idaho

True Stories of the Gem State's Most Infamous
Crooks, Culprits, and Cutthroats

Randy Stapilus

TWODOT®

GUILFORD, CONNECTICUT
HELENA, MONTANA
AN IMPRINT OF THE GLOBE PEQUOT PRESS

A · T W O D O T® · B O O K

Library of Congress Cataloging-in-Publication Data is available on file.

ISBN 978-0-7627-4374-2

Printed in the United States of America
10 9 8 7 6 5 4 3 2 1

To the people at the Idaho Historical Society, past and present, who helped with gathering the background and pictures for this book and for work I and others have done before. Idaho history would be lost without them.

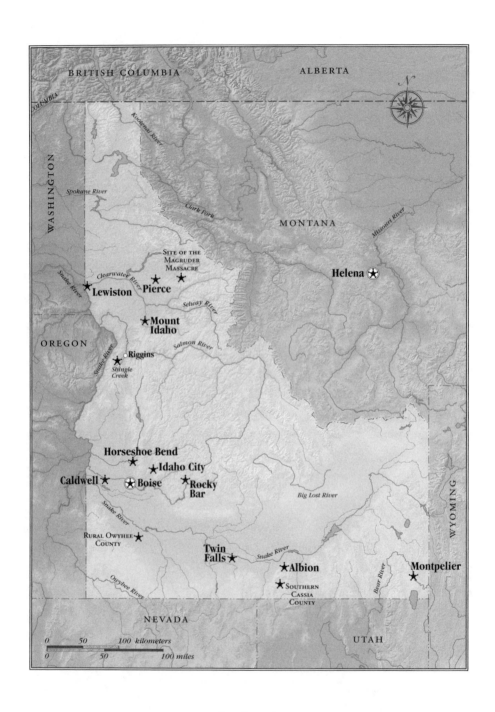

BRITISH COLUMBIA

ALBERTA

N

COLUMBIA

WASHINGTON

Spokane River

Kootenai River

Clark Fork

MONTANA

Missouri River

Helena ⊛

SITE OF THE
MAGRUDER
MASSACRE

Clearwater River

★
Pierce

★Lewiston

Snake River

Selway River

★Mount
Idaho

OREGON

Salmon River

★Riggins

Snake River

★
*Shingle
Creek*

Horseshoe Bend
★

★Idaho City

Caldwell ★

⊛★Boise

★Rocky
Bar

Big Lost River

WYOMING

Snake River

RURAL OWYHEE★
COUNTY

Twin
Falls★

Snake River

★Albion

Bear River

Montpelier
★

★SOUTHERN
CASSIA
COUNTY

Owyhee River

NEVADA

UTAH

0   50   100 *kilometers*

0   50   100 *miles*

I D A H O

Contents

Acknowledgments

This book would not have been what it is without help from a bunch of Idahoans.

First, collectively, everyone at the Idaho Historical Society provided great help. This is the prime source for information about Idaho history, and its new, more spacious building allows more room for storage—and improved prospects for locating key historical documents.

Judi Austin, who edited the *Idaho Yesterdays* magazine for the society for many years, is one of the core human resources any wise Idaho researcher will tap. Her suggestions and background (setting me on the track of the newly found Harry Orchard confession, for example) were invaluable.

Byron Johnson and Marty Peterson, who also provided important counsel, are two veterans of Idaho politics and government. Reciting their resumes would occupy a chapter at least; suffice it here to say that Johnson is a former state Supreme Court justice, Peterson is a former budget director and cities association leader and an advisor to the president of the University of Idaho, and both are passionate about Idaho history. Their advice on several chapters was very helpful.

And, of course, thanks to my wife Linda, whose support makes all my books possible.

Introduction

When Idaho Territory was created in 1863, it had the necessary raw material to become one of the great outlaw havens of the Western world. Its first American invaders were fast-buck miners, many of them on the run from the Civil War–era South, who set up prefabricated mining towns that rose and fell with startling speed. Money and gold moved hard and fast in these places; gunplay was frequent, robbery not unusual. Many of the people who came were Southern sympathizers during the time of the Civil War, and disputes between Unionists and the more numerous secessionists, or "seceshes," often led to bloodletting. Not till the 1870s did the territory, with developing farms and ranches and small cities, start to settle down.

But Idaho remained a frontier place for a long time. As late as 1900 the largest city in the state, Boise, numbered but eighteen thousand people. Established roads were few in the huge state, and law enforcement was spread thinly.

For all that, Idaho saw fewer than its share of the big-name Western outlaws, or lawmen for that matter. The biggest name on the side of the law to make himself an Idahoan was Wyatt Earp, but his stay can be measured in weeks, and he didn't come to enforce the law but to try to get rich. He was neither a sheriff nor a hired gun when he came, although he did have a kind of brush with the law. He arrived at the small mining boomtown of Eagle, north of the present-day Silver Valley, in 1884, together with brothers Warren and James; this was their first stop after leaving their far more famous haunts at Tombstone, Arizona. Warren and James bought a saloon called the White Elephant, and Wyatt bought several acres of land on which he planned some placer mining. Within weeks Wyatt Earp was sued by a man who said he owned the land—and Earp was evicted from it. The brothers left Idaho shortly thereafter.

Idaho developed some impressive law enforcement talent of its own, however, and one of the best-known lawmen in the area, Orlando "Rube" Robbins, became a figure of awe in the years before statehood, though his name is less known now, and not known much outside Idaho.

The only nationally known outlaw—that is, among outlaws still well known today—who we know plied his trade in Idaho was Butch Cassidy (without the Sundance Kid), and then only once, in the far southeast corner of the state. Most of his activities took place in Wyoming, Utah, and the Great Plains.

In his book *Idaho for the Curious,* writer Cort Conley described Hugh Whitney as "Idaho's best-known outlaw"—very possibly the best known that the Gem State produced before Prohibition. His was a dramatic career; the problem is that nearly all of it occurred outside Idaho.

He grew up in Brownlee, a community on the Snake River near where the Hells Canyon Dam now stands. He and his brothers were trained as shepherds, and in their middle teens in 1910 their parents sent them to Cokeville, Wyoming, to ply that trade. When Hugh's foreman fired him for trying to herd the sheep with a pistol and rifle, the teenager attacked him, and the foreman later died of his injuries. Hugh Whitney was arrested, then escaped. He and a brother fled to Montana, where rounds of shootings and robberies commenced. He robbed an Oregon Short Line train near Dubois, and was soon wanted by Idaho authorities, but that may have been his only major offense in his home state.

Eventually, Whitney and his brother Charley collected enough money to buy a ranch in Montana. Against the odds, Whitney stayed there, except for serving in the Army in World War I (under an assumed name), for the rest of his life, until 1951. Some time later Charley Whitney drove to Wyoming and confessed. He was pardoned, and finished his life at the ranch in Montana.

An amazing story in all, but mostly occurring outside Idaho.

More often than being a staging ground for crime sprees, Idaho has been a place of refuge. The last area of what was to become the United

States to be explored by Europeans, Idaho was also for many a kind of last chance to start over. For some, it worked. For others it didn't.

Idaho was en route to a combination of reputations for a fugitive named Henry Plummer (he spelled it Plumer, but the name is almost universally given the double *m* by others). Plummer's was a complex story, such a thorough mix of lawman and bad man that his name sparks debates even today, especially in western Montana, which is where he served as a marshal and also was lynched by vigilantes.

Plummer was a native of Maine who arrived in California with the gold rush and became sheriff at Nevada City. He apparently was energetic in upholding the law; he seems to have been no less energetic breaking it. He shot two men and engaged in various underhanded business schemes involving both mining and prostitution. Jailed in California after shooting a man (who had just stabbed him), he broke out and fled to Nevada, where he recuperated over the winter of 1861 to '62 in Carson City at the shack of Bill Mayfield, a friend of his. When the local sheriff came looking for Plummer, Mayfield stabbed him to death and had to run, choosing an even newer community, Walla Walla, Washington. Plummer soon joined him there, and before long they were met by an old friend of Mayfield's, Henry Talbott, better known as "Cherokee Bob." About the time of the next New Year's celebrations, Cherokee Bob managed to spark a riot and multiple killings in Walla Walla, and the three lit out of town again—for Idaho.

More specifically, they headed to Ragtown, as Lewiston was then known, named after the makeshift exterior walls on some of the buildings. Mayfield and Cherokee Bob, who were still being sought by Union troops for their part in the mess at Walla Walla, soon headed to the just-created boomtown of Florence, which was then—with nine thousand people—the second largest city in the northwest apart from Seattle, and flush with gold and cash. By way of threats and extortion, they wound up running a saloon there, and attracting the interest of "Red-haired Cynth," the estranged wife of another saloon operator in town. Cynth was their undoing; after Bob and Mayfield nearly came to a shootout over her (and Mayfield skipped town, and disappeared from history), Bob got into a shootout with her husband. Bad idea: Bob wound up full of holes.

Plummer had a longer history, long enough to play important roles, though mainly offstage, in two of the stories in this book, though he was an Idahoan for only a few months. Once in Idaho, he seems to have left most of his penchant for personal violence behind him, but he appears to have turned into a considerable criminal mastermind. He organized teams of "road agents"—highway robbers—who prowled the lightly traveled roads of the West. The effects of his efforts, even after his departure from Lewiston (where he spent only a few months) to Montana, were felt not only in the Lewiston Clearwater country, but as far south as the new town of Boise.

Idaho did not lack for outlaws. But most of them were homegrown, and were famous only regionally.

They cover a wide range of types—some of them truly as idiosyncratic as Idaho.

Some were true desperadoes—genuinely frightening and dangerous characters. Some extended their crookedness into corruption; both Idaho Territory's second governor and Boise city's first sheriff easily fit the description of outlaw, even if neither was brought to trial. (History has amply convicted both.) At least one was a man whose braggadocio led to tragedy; another was a man who made what may have been an impulsive mistake and made things worse trying to cover it up. The most cold-blooded of the group was a woman, and not a frontier figure at all, but a serial killer of her husbands.

Idaho continues to attract people who like to remove themselves from everyday society. Some of those people, now as in the past, live in remote crevasses, far from towns, and have as little to do with other people as possible. Most of them do, however, get along well enough with larger society when they happen to encounter it.

The dozen Idaho outlaws in the following pages did not fare quite so well.

The Magruder Incident

The high mountain sky was mostly blue, but dark gray clouds were rolling in; the brisk air required only the shelter of shirtsleeves, but the wind turned periodically chill. It was early October in the Bitterroot Mountains when the nine men made their way west on a barely visible trail.

They were six days out of Bannack, six days walking with their small pack train out of the valley and up into the mountains, a month later than most packers wanted to be traveling. The mountains were rugged, and the only good thing to say about their situation was that the range's divide—the highest point of their journey—was a couple of days behind them. They were into the Clearwater River basin now, but high up above the river, sloshing through the thinnest of its headwaters from time to time. Snow sometimes fell up here in October, and the nine men were eager to move on.

Apart from that, the agendas of the nine men were not all the same.

The pack leader was Lloyd Magruder, a businessman who lived in Lewiston—a hundred miles or so west—now returning from dropping off a large pack train of supplies in the Montana mining camps. Most of his crew remained in Bannack or Virginia City, but his chief packer, Charles Allen, was headed back with him.

They had not wanted to make the risky trek alone, so they threw out a net for other men to accompany them. Fellow packer Bill Phillips was also headed west—either to Lewiston or Walla Walla. Two brothers, named Chalmers, were a pair of runabouts looking for work. The youngest of the bunch was Billy Page, a teenaged adventure seeker returning to his digs in Walla Walla. Three other rough-looking characters, who seemed to have knocked around the West but whose backgrounds were a little mysterious, were David Renton, Christopher Lower, and James Romain.

1

Magruder, who knew the way better than the others, was satisfied with their progress. The sun started its slip behind the mountains ahead, and as the group rounded its way into a clearing, bounded by a ravine on one side and a low cliff on the other, Magruder called a halt and announced that they'd camp here for the night.

Allen, less familiar with this path than Magruder but aware of mountain weather, pulled out his tent. "We'll have snow in the morning," he declared. Magruder looked pensive; the others all said Allen was overreacting, tossed out their bedrolls, and started a couple of campfires. They set the horses to graze on the far side of the clearing.

Darkness was falling by the time they'd finished eating. Magruder, puffing his pipe, was still mulling over the weather. He had agreed to take the first shift on guard, together with Lower. They walked into the forest, Magruder with his rifle and Lower with an ax, to gather more wood. They returned and piled it on the fires. Magruder caught a glimpse of the kid, Billy Page, watching this activity—he seemed to have a case of the nerves, no telling about what.

Magruder put it out of his mind as the night wore on. He and Lower talked by the fire, and then Renton, who said he'd had trouble getting to sleep, joined them. The night was silent but for the crackling of the fire and the softly spoken words of the men around it.

Renton remarked that the fire needed more wood and offered to cut some more. Lower stood up, grabbed his ax, and said he'd join him. Magruder nodded and leaned forward to light his pipe by the fire.

At that moment, Lower swung the flat of his ax and smashed it through the back of Magruder's skull, smacking his head forward into the fire. Magruder died instantly. But Renton grabbed the ax and swung it down on Magruder's head again, just to make sure.

That was the start of the killing.

Renton gestured to Romain—the third in his group—and they walked over to Page, who was awake and wide-eyed. "You awake?" Renton asked.

Page, in near-shock, nodded.

"Good," he said, "stay there."

It's happening, Page thought as he lay there, frozen in place. Lower had hinted a few days before that this would happen, and he hadn't believed it. Now he was lying in the middle of a killing ground.

Romain and Renton walked softly to where the Chalmers brothers slept, and each brought an ax head down on one of the brothers. After a few muffled groans, they were gone.

They slipped back near Page, where Phillips was asleep, and smashed in his skull.

That left Allen, sleeping in his tent. This called for a change of tactics, so Renton ducked back to his bedroll, grabbed his shotgun, made his way to Allen's tent, and shot through it—blowing off part of Allen's head.

Apart from the three killers, only Page was left. Romain walked over to him. "You're scared," he observed. "You're all atremble." No need to worry, he said: "All the dirty work is done."

North-central Idaho is rugged, challenging country, almost entirely mountainous. Even today it remains lightly settled, and few roads traverse it. The stretch of U.S. Highway 12 that passes through Idaho—which travelers drive from Lewiston on the west border of Idaho to Lolo, Montana, just past the east border—was completed only in the 1960s. South or north of that, the next highway system running east-west is more than a hundred miles away. But there is also one very rough, unpaved, and difficult backcountry road, a pathway running along the thin gap between the Frank Church River of No Return Wilderness and the Selway-Bitterroot Wilderness. It is sometimes hiked or bicycled, and occasionally driven with great care in motor vehicles, but it is so rough that it is not usually described as a road. Most people, and even official government publications, call it the Magruder Corridor.

It was named for Lloyd Magruder, a Lewiston man, one of the city's first businessmen. Modern-day travelers struggling along the corridor can at least take heart that their experience on the road is better than his.

Magruder brought his wife and children from California to Lewiston in 1862. Down in California, he had heard all about the spectacular new gold fields up north, at Pierce and Orofino. He was ambitious but not grasping, rather a steadier, more stolid figure than the mining country usually attracted. Magruder had little interest in mining, but he knew if miners were nearby, they would need a place to spend their money.

Sensing opportunity in the new town of Lewiston, a kind of base camp for the miners in the Clearwater River country, he decided to set up as a merchant and shipper of general goods, as he had in California. By his first fall there, he watched the Clearwater River gold fields at Pierce and Orofino dwindle rapidly, and the booming mining communities almost collapsed.

But Lewiston itself didn't suffer, largely because new mining fields were sprouting still further east, much further, over the Bitterroot Mountains in what is now Montana, centered around a quickly sprung town called Bannack. Although it was more than 150 miles away, Lewiston was the best available supply center for the Montana mines, and by the spring of 1863 several Lewiston packers, Magruder among them, were making money hauling flour, food, whiskey, and other supplies from Lewiston to Bannack over a very rough Indian trail.

It was a slight trail, difficult for hikers and even tougher for pack animals, climbing to seven thousand feet in some places. Magruder's team had a sixty-mule train, and about two dozen packers.

The heat of August had arrived, but everyone knew that in the higher reaches, snow would begin falling in September, while the team would probably still be on its way back. Magruder was determined to make one more run, though, and packed his train to leave in mid-August.

Send-off from Lewiston was an event. Most of Lewiston's children were there to watch, along with many of the business owners, and Magruder's wife.

Magruder's friend Hill Beachey, owner of the new Lewiston hotel called the Luna House, walked up shortly before departure. Husky but energetic—he was often described as "hyperactive"—Beachey showed up with a present: a new rifle, which he pressed on Magruder, who at first said he wouldn't need it. Beachey didn't tell Magruder the reason for his urgency, but he would tell people in town over the days to come: The night before, he'd dreamed that Magruder had been attacked and killed out in the wilderness.

The trip east unfolded efficiently. Magruder stopped at Fort Lapwai, where he dined with the commander of the fort, an old friend. He avoided the old Pierce and Orofino mining camps but passed through a couple of Indian encampments, where he engaged in some light trading. The pack train pulled in for supplies at Elk City, a small mining encampment, and there he was surprised to find a letter addressed to him. It was signed by the Nez Perce County Democrats, who were casting about for a candidate for the new territorial congressional seat. Magruder had been elected to office before, as clerk of Yuba County, California. He was popular enough in Lewiston to be a credible prospect, and the Democrats asked him his views on the issues of the day, especially on the Lincoln Administration. Magruder, a native Marylander who had lived for years in the South, had no use for the Lincoln Administration, and said so. He posted his reply and headed east in a good mood. Then, tracing the Clearwater River back to its headwaters, he and the pack train began the long climb up into the Bitterroot Mountains. Working steadily, they managed about ten to fifteen miles a day.

Magruder's mood darkened when the train arrived at Bannack. One reason was that the gold boom, running so strong only a few months before, already had petered out. Because of this the town was depopulating. But Magruder was also bothered by something else—the new sheriff at Bannock. He knew him, and really wished he didn't. His name was Henry Plummer.

Hill Beachey, owner of the Luna House
Courtesy Idaho State Historical Society

In a time and place where people had arrived but the law was still struggling to catch up, Plummer walked every side of the fence. Too ambitious to stay home in New England, he arrived in California just behind the curve of the gold rush. Unable to cash in on the easy finds, but charismatic and more cultured than most of the new Californians, Plummer was elected a town marshal.

He held the position only briefly, soon shooting and killing two men for no lawful reason, which led to a stretch at San Quentin. Seeking a new start, Plummer moved north and scouted prospects around the north Idaho gold fields. In July 1862, a year earlier, Plummer had checked into Hill Beachey's Luna House, and Beachey and Magruder had taken note of the unsavory types—with rustling, robbing, and killing histories—with whom Plummer hung out. Plummer seemed to be setting himself up for another run at elective office, but his reputation was poor in Lewiston. He soon moved on to Bannack; Beachey and Magruder were glad to see him go.

At Bannack, Plummer met more old acquaintances, with different results this time. In the bars he ran into a man named Cleveland, whom he had known and collided with in California. One night, Cleveland went out of his way to attack Plummer and a woman he was with in a bar. Plummer did not let it go. Days later, in another bar, Plummer shot Cleveland dead. The Bannack sheriff investigating the incident figured Plummer for a bad actor and, on the street, took a shot at him and hit him in the arm. Having failed to kill Plummer, the sheriff quit town, and Plummer was elected sheriff to replace him.

Magruder quickly made his way through Bannack and headed on to Virginia City, which he'd heard was the place with the newest gold boom. His information was correct, and once he connected with the people in town he did a bustling business there. But the extra travel and extra negotiating time had cost him. The calendar now read mid-September, and the road home, over those 7,000-foot elevations, would be difficult and dangerous. Most of his original pack crew, finding the mining opportunities good at Virginia City, decided to winter there, or maybe stay longer. Magruder cut most of his pack loose and, at the end of September, started back with only his chief packer, Charles Allen.

And $18,000, mostly in gold dust.

Because of the gold, a 150-mile run to Lewiston by so small a number of travelers—only two men, bringing back several horses, equipment, and valuables—was risky. So Magruder scouted around Bannack to add new men to bulk up his traveling group to a sturdier size. In the case of three of his additions, he chose poorly.

Money, when it weighed down a pocket as heavily as Magruder's, did not long stay a secret in the mining camps. Before long Plummer, the sheriff at Bannack, was well apprised. Pondering the opportunity, he was also considering what to do about three ne'er-do-wells who had settled in at Bannack: David Renton, Christopher Lower, and James Romain. He decided to solve both problems at once: He told the three about the money headed west on the Indian trail, and settled back to await his share of the loot. Unless the three decided to run, in which case he'd deal with them later.

The three, together with a young tagalong named Billy Page, who was unaware of their plans, linked up with Magruder and Allen, along with three others—two brothers named Chalmers, and a packer named Bill Phillips—who were glad to have additional men to fortify their expedition. They left Bannack on October 3 and headed west, just as winter season was preparing to hit in the high mountains.

The group had good weather as they climbed the Bitterroots, and within three days they were over the heights and into the Clearwater Valley. They encountered two horsemen headed in the opposite direction, but no one else. This was open wilderness, with no people around.

Three days into the trip, after making camp, Lower pulled Page aside and told him Magruder was carrying $18,000 in gold, and he, Renton, and Romain meant to have it. That would probably mean killing. "If you value your life," he said, "stay alert but keep quiet."

A couple of nights later, deep in the wilderness, came the killings.

Job one was cleaning up after the killings. Renton brought out four pairs of moccasins, and insisted that the killers wear them; this way, Indians probably would be blamed for the killings. He and his associates dragged away the bodies and dumped them down the ravine, while Page gathered belongings and equipment that would no longer be needed and threw them in the fire.

Page didn't know the mountains well, and along the way the four encountered heavy rain and snow. But in the early evening of October 18, taking back roads into town to avoid being seen, they finally reached Lewiston.

Their destination was the Pacific coast, but so late in the season they would need organized transportation. Renton tried to hire a boat to run downstream on the Snake River, but none could be found. He dispatched Lower to find a stage to take them west, and now they made a mistake. Lower walked into the main stage sales office, which was in the Luna House—owned and operated by Magruder's friend Hill Beachey.

Lower was not the sharpest criminal in the West, and he tripped up several times as he arranged for four stage tickets. He sounded especially suspicious when he was asked to supply the names of the four passengers—he hadn't expected to have to make them up on the spot. Lower finally got the tickets and left. But Beachey had witnessed some of the conversation. Magruder was much overdue for his return, and the surprise appearance of four men with money, just arrived from the wilderness to the east, struck him as suspicious.

Early the next morning he tried to talk the sheriff into holding up the departure of the stage, but the sheriff thought the evidence was too slight. It left with the four men, but Beachey continued to nose around, talking to people who had been in the Clearwater region and had reports from Bannack. His suspicions started to grow, and the sheriff agreed to appoint him as a deputy so he could try to bring back the four mystery men for questioning.

The pursuit was frustrating at first. Along with a friend, Thomas Farrell, Beachey rode on horseback to Portland, the stage's destination. There he just missed the four, who had taken a ship south to San Francisco after enjoying themselves and spending part of their loot. Working with law enforcement in Portland, Beachey sent word by high-speed messenger south to San Francisco. By the time Beachey arrived, the local police had arrested all four and were holding them for return to Lewiston.

Beachey found that he had one more tough job when he returned to Lewiston. A lynch mob had formed and tried to seize the four defendants. Beachey was able to get them into jail, insisting they should be tried properly.

And they were. Page agreed to turn evidence against the other three and supplied many of the details about what had happened out in the wilderness. The others, David Renton, Christopher Lower, and James Romain, were convicted of murder and were hanged at Lewiston in March 1864.

Beachey himself had begun to sour on Lewiston. That November he sold the Luna House and moved with his family south to Nevada, where he would take up business, and die about a decade hence.

But before he could leave, Beachey had one last job to do. In May 1864, accompanied by about a dozen other Lewistonians, he rode out along the Magruder trail. Following clues from Page's testimony—which the physical evidence appeared to bear out—they found the site of the murders. They found the remains of the bodies, the cups that held hot coffee just before the killings, the remnants of Magruder's pack equipment—enough to confirm Page's version of events.

Beachey had wanted to hold the trial partly so that the truth could be told and Magruder's killing documented. All that had happened. Now, he suggested, it should be memorialized. There is no longer—as there once was—a sign to mark the exact spot of the Magruder murders.

But the travelers along the Magruder corridor memorialize it to this day.

The Opportunist

Caleb Lyon was not an unfamiliar sight at the territorial Indian Affairs office—as governor of the territory he was also the Indian Affairs commissioner. In his elegant suits, his perfectly coiffed goatee, and his poetic if patrician manner, he was as unmistakable as he was familiar—to a great many Idahoans, altogether too familiar. But on this day his smooth patter and deft assurances still didn't entirely satisfy the clerk, who was unsure why the governor needed to personally withdraw $50,000 in cash from the federal receipts.

"The tribes," he said, "have to be paid. They are getting impatient."

This didn't sound right, as Lyon usually preferred that tribal leaders come to him, not the other way around. Not only that, Lyon had dispensed money before, and this was not the procedure he had used.

The clerk resisted, and suggested that Lyon's successor take care of it. Even in this remote place, hundreds of miles from the nearest telegraph, word had arrived that Lyon was soon to be replaced by a political appointee named David Ballard.

"Who knows when Ballard will get here," Lyon insisted, and then walked out with $50,000.

Days later, he took the stage south and made his way to San Francisco. He stayed there several months, through the winter, then boarded a ship for the long journey around the Americas. By the time he arrived in New York, Ballard and others had checked over the books at Indian Affairs and had questions for Lyon.

Soon after he disembarked at New York, federal inspectors tracked him down and began the interrogation. Lyon told them he had never seen the money. His patter was smooth enough that they went on their way, thinking someone must have been mistaken.

Agents eventually caught up with Lyon in Washington, D.C., and

11

Caleb Lyon
Courtesy Idaho State Historical Society

questioned him further. Lyon's new story was that he had taken the best care of the money. He watched it day and night. On the train from New York to Washington, he took a sleeper car and kept the money under his pillow. And the night before he arrived in Washington—it was stolen. Somebody robbed him.

It was a story not many eastern government officials were inclined to believe. Something about the western territories seemed to bring out the worst in political appointees with sticky fingers. For many years Nevada was called the "rotten borough" for its corruption in the 1800s, but to its north the Idaho Territory matched Nevada's reputation. The few government officials Idaho Territory had in its earliest days were given little money either from the federal government or from local taxpayers, but what little there was managed to find its way mostly into the pockets of shady dealers.

One of them was Alfred Slocum, who became treasurer of Boise County (which did not include Boise but was based around the busy mining towns northeast of there). In 1864 his office managed to collect $14,000 in property taxes. The next year, the territorial government demanded he turn most of it over, as the law required. Slocum refused, offering one excuse after another. For one thing, he said, money was needed to run the county jail; but that didn't amount to much, since the "jail" was a barnlike building that held no one who chose to leave.

Furthermore, he noted that two men were each claiming to be the treasurer of Idaho Territory, so he didn't know whom to pay. Slocum said he wanted the matter settled in court. Actually, he wanted it to go away, since (as territorial officials learned later) Slocum had embezzled the money and already spent most of it. When he was found out, a long legal battle ensued covering two trials, one hung jury, and an attempt to escape to Oregon. Eventually, Slocum served prison time.

Caleb Lyon, who liked to call himself "Caleb Lyon of Lyonsdale," never served time in prison, but that seems to have been not for want of effort but because he was just slippery enough, and he had a gift for talking his way out of problems.

He came from money and prominence; "Lyonsdale" actually was an estate in northern New York, and the Lyon family had some inherited money along with political and business contacts. Caleb was given the appropriate advantages, was sent to boarding school in Montreal and university in Vermont, and went off for several years to complete his real-world education in Europe, where he spent several years traveling. He began writing, with mixed results, an almost baroque poetry and an odd novel about a British traveler who fell into the hands of the Aborigines of Tasmania. He occasionally lectured around the eastern states as well. Lyon made no great waves but he cut an unusual figure, dressing atypically for the day; for a while he was best known for his velvet coat, red cravat, and shoulder-length hair—definitely not in style in the 1840s.

With family money at his back, he might have stayed in those circles, but apparently he was given the impression from family members that he should at least make a show of entering a career. With his gift for speaking and making connections, he soon made his way to politics.

The opening came from his father, who was active in Democratic politics and a personal friend of William Marcy, who was secretary of state in the Polk Administration. In 1844 a treaty was signed with China providing, among other things, that an American consul would be stationed at the Chinese city of Shanghai. Marcy gave the job to his friend's son Caleb. What Caleb Lyon did with the job is unclear; the available records seem to suggest that he never crossed the Pacific, and that when he resigned in 1849 at the end of the Polk Administration, he had never set foot in Shanghai. Maybe it was just as well; Lyon considered himself a Whig, not a Democrat.

Two decades later, just before he was to become governor of Idaho, Lyon claimed he had spent the mid-1840s as an Army officer, traveling with General Winfield Scott in the Mexican War. Searches of military records from that period found no reference to him, and he seems to have made up the story.

When he surfaced in 1849 to turn in his resignation as consul, he was in California. The next year, in Sacramento, he talked his way into the job of secretary of the constitutional convention of the state-to-be; he apparently executed that job. But when he presented to the convention a proposed state seal, which a grateful convention paid him $1,000 for designing, he apparently failed to mention that he'd plagiarized it: It was actually designed by someone else.

Returning to New York, Lyon leveraged his gift for self-promotion first into a term in the state Senate and then two terms in the U.S. House. After he lost the House seat in 1856, his family's mansion burned and money became tighter, and Lyon migrated to Washington to look for another appointed job.

After Abraham Lincoln's election in 1860, the politics were right for Lyon—he had made the transition from Whig to Independent to Republican, much as Lincoln had—but he had to wait his turn. Over the next couple of years, as the Civil War intensified, stories circulated about Lyon as a Union military leader (some of them suggesting he had enriched himself in the position), but he never wore a uniform in this war, either.

Courtesy of a connection to Lincoln's interior secretary, Lyon got the appointment in early 1864 as governor of Idaho Territory, a jurisdiction created less than a year before and which Lyon had never visited. There was opposition. The outgoing (and first) governor, William Wallace, who had resigned to become Idaho's delegate in Congress, advised Lincoln to appoint someone else. And word from back in New York, notably from influential Republican Roscoe Conkling, was less than supportive; Conkling specifically questioned Lyon's "moral character." But Lyon was confirmed by the Senate in February 1864.

He did not speed his way west. He stayed in New York until June. Then, having hired the interior secretary's son as a personal assistant, he sailed around South America to Portland, and arrived in Lewiston, the territorial capital of Idaho, in August. He hired the services of Wells Fargo to move his books and other major supplies, and told them to bill the federal government—which refused to pay. Wells Fargo apparently was never compensated.

In his first report back, Lyon wrote, "I commence the administration of this Department under difficulties of the gravest description." This time, Lyon told the literal truth. The territory, little more than a year old, was already $44,000 in debt, and no sources of financial help were obvious. Lyon had no law enforcement and no territory marshal to call upon. The territory was flooded with antiwar Democrats who had no use for any kind of Republican. As governor, Lyon was superintendent of Indian Affairs, and the Indian tribes in the territory, mainly the Nez Perce and the Shoshoni, were complaining that federal treaty obligations for money, supplies, and more had not been fulfilled. Lyon did learn, however, a little about the Nez Perce treaty lands. He sent a confidential letter to the interior secretary urging that the treaty with the tribe be amended to exclude a specific tract of land with valuable minerals on it—so that he and the secretary could swoop in and buy it.

There were more problems. Many of the residents wanted to split the territory between north and south, and those in the south wanted the capital moved to the new town of Boise. In the fall of 1864, Lyon traveled south to the Boise area and the new mining territory there, and concluded the obvious: This would be the site of most new population and economic growth. He publicly backed moving the territorial capital from Lewiston to Boise, and when the legislature convened in December at Lewiston and passed a bill to do just that, Lyon signed it.

Lewistonians didn't take the news well. The next February they filed a lawsuit seeking to throw out all of the actions of the last legislative session, and got a court order to require Lyon to stay at Lewiston. He wanted to leave, fast, fearing that Lewiston was becoming a dangerous place for him. So he told people he was heading to the Snake River to hunt ducks, but instead, once out of sight, crossed to the other side, joined a buggy he'd sent ahead, and raced for his life to Walla Walla, not stopping for long until he had crossed the continent completely the other way and returned in the spring to Washington, D.C.

In the months that followed, the territorial capital was moved south to Boise, but the work of the territory slowed to a crawl, except for one thing. Early in 1865, about the time Lyon was hightailing out of the territory, Congress finally agreed to send money west for the operation of Idaho Territory—$33,000 for salaries and other expenses. More money, to meet the terms of the Indian treaties, would soon be coming and thus was awaiting recovery by a proper Idaho official.

The highest official in the territory at the moment was a private secretary. Lyon's territorial assistant, DeWitt Smith—who had been left holding the bag at Lewiston—had died, and his secretary, a former San Francisco bartender named Horace Gilson, was more or less in charge. After raiding the accounts of his now-dead boss, he made friends with territorial businessmen and looked for other funds. When he heard about the $33,000 at Oregon City, he arranged the necessary paperwork to pick it up. A few months later, he said that he needed to go to San Francisco to negotiate a printing contract for the territory. Neither Gilson nor the $33,000 was ever seen again.

When officials back in Washington found out the money they had sent for the tribes was gone, they were furious, and the seeds of investigation were planted. But one of the first things they did was to pull out more money from the federal treasury and send it west to Idaho.

Using his smooth-talking ways, Lyon turned back several efforts in Washington to fire him from the governor's office. Lyon returned to Idaho, arriving just a few weeks ahead of the second round of federal payments. While in Washington, he had interested investors in a railroad scheme to connect the Portland area with the East, and pushed a special bill through the territorial legislature.

But by then, much of his attention, and the territory's, was focused on the increasing anger and discontent among the Indian tribes, which still were not receiving the annuities they had been promised. In the fall of 1865, Oregon senator James Nesmith began looking into the Indian bureau's accounts. With the turn of the New Year, he accused Lyon of having "shamefully neglected" his work with the tribes, and having failed to keep many of the accounting records for the money.

The investigation continued, and general criticism from within Idaho continued to reach Washington. After Lincoln was assassinated and Andrew Johnson, a Democrat, took over as president, Lyon lost his source of political support. In April 1866 Johnson sent word that Lyon was dismissed, his place to be taken by an Oregonian, David Ballard. Lyon headed back to San Francisco, but his Idaho story was not over.

Nesmith advised Ballard to keep looking into the records of the Indian Affairs office, and soon, that summer, they found what they had suspected—a $50,000 discrepancy between the amounts Lyon said he had received and the amounts he said he had given to the tribes. His first response was that he'd never had the money.

Communication was slow in those days, and the federal department heads threatened to take Lyon to court to squeeze the money out of him. Lyon took his time in San Francisco and finally returned to New York in the spring of 1867. Asked what happened to the $50,000, Lyon coolly replied that he'd had it with him when he left Idaho, and that he'd planned to turn it in to the appropriate federal officials. He had it with him, he said, on a train headed to Washington. He said he had kept it under his pillow. But from under his pillow, he said, someone had stolen it while Lyon slept.

Lyon was never prosecuted; his trial probably would have been a big embarrassment to too many prominent people. The money was mostly recovered from the bonding company that had insured Lyon. But Lyon's political fortunes never recovered; he retired quietly in New York, where he died in 1875.

On hearing of that news, the *Idaho Statesman* in Boise remarked that he ought to have died in prison.

A Civil War Reenactment

The summer Sunday was bright and almost glaring at Idaho City, and about a mile south of Main Street on the road to Boise, the afternoon had turned sultry. The warm springs just south of town—an easier, more relaxing bath than the hotter springs to the north—had drawn only a few people so far this day, though the saloon in front, between the Boise Road and the pools, was about half full.

The drinkers within had felt surly for weeks. Some of them were Southerners, expatriates from the now-beaten Confederacy, surrendered at Appomattox three months before. Nearly all the rest of the clientele sympathized with them. Just about all were glad Abe Lincoln was no more. This was a Democratic mining town, and Republicans were not welcome.

So they startled when they heard a clear, strong voice outside, a couple of clomping horses bringing it ever closer, ever louder, singing the hated tune (to the music of "The Battle Hymn of the Republic"):

> *The stars in Heaven are looking kindly down,*
> *The stars in Heaven are looking kindly down,*
> *The stars in Heaven are looking kindly down,*
> *On the grave of old John Brown.*

The singing paused, and then the singer strolled in—a big, confident, cocky smile on his face. They all knew him. It was Ol' Pink himself—Sumner Pinkham—till recently a U.S. marshal and more recently a candidate for sheriff. He was a Unionist, and a Republican, and he was rubbing it in.

He got to the bar, ordered a drink, smiled to his friend, and kept right on singing.

Ol' Pink, otherwise known as Sumner Pinkham

Courtesy Idaho State Historical Society

We'll hang Jeff Davis to a sour apple tree,
We'll hang Jeff Davis to a sour apple tree,
We'll hang Jeff Davis to a sour apple tree,
As we go marching on.

Pinkham smiled again and looked around. But he drew little reaction. The bar's patrons weren't going to give him the satisfaction.

He and his friend sat down with their drinks. They sat there a while and chatted, but the glares from all around got to be too much for them, even for Pinkham, a man known to enjoy infuriating everyone else in a room. So they stood up and headed for the door, the idea being to finish their drinks on the front porch.

As they hit the door, they came face to face with Ferd Patterson.

The silence went from uneasy to deadly.

The two men had a history. It went back to Pinkham's days as a marshal, when some of his most energetic work had to do with Patterson. It also had to do with the political polarities of Boise: Patterson was as ardent a Democrat and Confederate as Pinkham was a Republican and Unionist.

When they met at the door, they looked each other in the eye and ran through the quick inventory—*he's armed, I'm armed.* (Some people later said Patterson had arrived at the warm springs unarmed.) By some unspoken agreement, it seemed, the rivals determined this was not the time or place. They made their way past each other, Pinkham to drink on the front veranda with his friend, Patterson to do likewise in the saloon.

After some drinks in the saloon, Patterson walked out back to the swimming pools. He sat around there for a while, talking with friends, probably enjoying the late afternoon weather. And the drinking continued, steadily.

He would say later that he was trying to forget who was on the front porch, and was trying to outwait him—hoping Pinkham would leave first. But every so often, that big singing voice would erupt again, and Patterson would know he was still there.

21

The fury increased.

Patterson had another drink. Then, finally, he'd had enough.

He was not alone, as the crowd in the saloon badly wanted to smack that smirk off Sumner Pinkham's face, and who better to do it than Ferd Patterson?

The saloonkeeper waved him over to the bar and reached down behind it. He pulled out a rifle. "Here," he said, "you can use this."

The saloonkeeper had a secret. He wanted no fighting or killing on his premises, and the powder keg he saw before him needed only the tiniest spark. The gun, he knew, wouldn't work. He had left the rifle out in the elements, out in the snow, all winter—had forgotten it was there—and it was ruined now. He had inspected it not long ago, and it was spoiled—choked with rust, pieces almost falling apart.

Patterson, who was skilled with guns and knew something about rifles, had had enough drinks that he didn't notice.

He ambled to the front door, pushed through, and peered out onto the front porch. Sumner Pinkham was still there, talking with his friend. He paused to look over at Patterson. His right hand moved south, toward his gun belt—he certainly was armed.

Ferdinand Patterson, a little shakily, rose to his full six feet, stalked to within a man's height of Pinkham and spat out at him: "You will draw on me, will you?"

He pulled up his rifle, aimed it, and pulled the rusty trigger.

And it fired.

Pinkham's body, probably dead before it hit solid ground, flew off the front of the porch, twelve feet down into Warm Creek, which ran in front of the porch.

The next thing the people at the saloon saw was a small cloud of dust to the north—Patterson was riding off, as fast as he could go.

The shooting of Sumner Pinkham by Ferdinand Patterson at the Idaho City warm springs on July 23, 1865, was not a surprise. People around Idaho City had expected it for some time; the issue was when and where, not if. But who was right and what it meant—there was the rub, a rub touchy enough to bring two mobs face to face, just short of starting a small civil war in the largest city in Idaho.

The storm had been building for two years. Or longer.

Ferd Patterson grew up in Alabama—we do not know if he was born there—and took his social cues from the southern aristocracy of the place. He grew tall, probably more than six feet, and wore a curved mustache that gave him a distinguished look. He had an impressive, serious mien; he might have managed a career in politics but instead latched onto gambling. Two other things came with him out of Alabama: a deep attachment to the states' rights and Democratic politics of his home, and a hair-trigger, sometimes lethal, temper. Drinking was said to worsen his temper, and most of his violent incidents happened in or around saloons.

He left Alabama for Texas and then left Texas for California. He was drawn, along with so many others, to the California gold fields of the Sacramento area. Soon enough, he plied his gambling skill at separating overconfident miners from their finds and became moderately prosperous. He dressed stylishly, wore a gold watch and chain, and walked with a trendy cane.

When the Civil War cracked open, California turned sharply from a Democratic state with some sympathy for the South to a Republican, pro-Union place. That may have been part of the reason that in late 1862, Patterson booked one-way passage on a ship headed north to Portland for himself and his mistress, a long-haired blonde beauty who instantly attracted plenty of attention. On arriving in Portland, he learned that the captain of the ship, staying in the same hotel he was, had taken notice of the couple and, in loud barroom talk, was denouncing him as a Southern traitor. That pulled the hair trigger; Patterson grabbed the pistol from his room, ran down the stairs, and shot and killed the captain.

Patterson was arrested and jailed. He managed to clear himself by claiming he had shot the captain in self-defense. But then his hair trigger was pulled again when he found his mistress, back at the hotel, with another man. This time he put down his pistol and grabbed a Bowie knife, and started hacking the blonde tresses from his mistress. In the process, he became overeager: He explained later in an Idaho saloon, "My knife slipped, and the blade, I reckon, cut a little too deep."

He was arrested again, and immediately posted the $500 bail. And then, as the *Idaho Tri-Weekly Statesman* would soon put it, he "left for some other city where there is no penitentiary"—but where, it might also have noted, there were plenty of Southern sympathizers.

He could hardly have chosen better than the new mining boomtowns of Idaho.

First stop was a city less than eighteen months old that would be, within a few years, a ghost town: Florence, in north-central Idaho northeast of what is now Riggins. There he found an environment much like that of the mining communities of northern California, with two differences. It was more rugged and temporary. But, offsetting that, the miners were overwhelmingly Southerners or Southern sympathizers, and by the time Patterson arrived they had already heard tales about how he had defended the cause back in Portland.

Patterson became cockier in Florence. With some Southern friends, he decided to take over a new local brewery, and not through arm's-length negotiations. The aggrieved owner and others in town called on the U.S. marshal to do something, and the marshal did—he threw Patterson in jail. That marked the first run-in between Patterson and the marshal, whose name was Sumner Pinkham.

Pinkham and Patterson saw in each other everything they each loathed. Patterson was slippery, corrupt, and crooked by nature, and liked living that way; Pinkham tended to self-righteousness. Patterson organized crime; Pinkham did what he could to break it up. Most especially, Pinkham was a Northerner—a native of Maine, raised in

Wisconsin—and an ardent Unionist Republican. Their meetings were especially combustible because of what they had in common. They were both powerfully built men, and both skillful with firearms. Both liked to dominate a room, and both reacted swiftly to a challenge. Pinkham was a little older, and his thick white beard seemed to add still more years. Pinkham had some background as a gambler, but he had moved on to throw in with law enforcement. And he had a temper that easily matched Patterson's.

Both of them liked to be provocative.

That summer of 1863, the gold mines of Florence were dying out, and the mining community there began to scatter. Idaho also became a territory, and law enforcement was about to be increased. Pinkham left Florence for Idaho City to the south, there to become the Boise County sheriff, at least until an election would be held the next year. Patterson, hearing about the next big mining town forming at Idaho City, took the same route. Organizing his fellow Southerners, he helped defeat Pinkham when the office of sheriff came up for election.

As the last of the ballots were being counted, as Patterson was celebrating on the main street of Idaho City, he came face to face with Sumner Pinkham, who was worked up into a rage. There was no discussion; there was nothing to say. Pinkham simply twisted a bit to the side and swung, a legendarily powerful, smashing blow to the jaw, throwing Ferd Patterson almost off the street and into the gutter on the side. The audience, quickly grown in the space of a minute, was silenced, and did not interfere as Sumner Pinkham walked off. Patterson's friends discouraged him from chasing after, and helped him back to his rooms.

Patterson had the rest of the night to recuperate and consider. When the next day he emerged on the street, he did not do what many in Idaho City expected, which was to hunt down and kill Sumner Pinkham. Instead he emerged coatless, in his shirtsleeves, showing that he was unarmed and not seeking a fight. He stayed that way for a few more days.

And then, saying he had to visit his dying mother in Illinois, Sumner Pinkham rode out of town.

In the year that followed, Idaho City prospered, and so did Ferd Patterson. He became a popular leader in town among the Southern sympathizers, a role that did not diminish even as word reached Idaho that the Confederacy's days were over. For a time, about 20,000 miners packed into the Boise River basin mountains near Idaho City and, briefly, the gold mining was good. Patterson's ways had not changed, but they fit smoothly into the scene.

Then one day in July of 1865, a few months after Appomattox, as Southern sensitivities reached their peak, Sumner Pinkham returned to Idaho City.

Word spread from one end of Idaho City to the other. A low buzz ran through the town, and the message was consistent. Sometime in the days ahead, Ferd Patterson and Sumner Pinkham were going to have it out.

The first words anyone heard from Ferd Patterson after he had shot Pinkham were spoken about fourteen miles southwest of Idaho City on the road to Boise, at the small Star Road House run by Frank and Hester Davis. Patterson had not had sufficient time to calm himself. He was tearing up the road as he jumped off his horse and approached Frank Davis. From a distance he hollered, "Frank—Frank—I shot Pinkham at Warm Springs. Quick—give me a blanket and something to eat. I must cut off into the hills."

Hester Davis said later (in a signed statement) that her husband promptly brought a blanket while she prepared a lunch for Patterson to take along in his saddlebag. He rode off, but only minutes later "we saw five or six men coming on horseback, not in the road but over the hills. They hollered, 'Got any fresh horses?' and 'How long since Ferd came?'" They were led by the sheriff—Jack Gorman, whom Patterson had helped elect—and Deputy Rube Robbins.

Orlando "Rube" Robbins would go on to become one of the legendary lawmen of Idaho Territory. He had been all around the mining camps, gradually moving himself into law enforcement, and had some experience by the time of the Pinkham shooting. But this was his first big capture. That same evening he led the final surround of the road house, still shy of Boise, where the sheriff's posse finally caught up with Patterson. They started back to Idaho City, intending to lock Patterson in the Boise County jail. Charged with the murder of a former sheriff, he seemed unlikely to escape easily this time.

That was where Idaho's own civil war almost began.

Gorman and his deputies got advance word that the road back to Idaho City was lined with people, most of whom, for one reason or another, had come to hate Patterson or befriend Pinkham. Taking a back trail through the mountains, they made their way into Idaho City from behind, slipped into the courthouse, and barricaded themselves inside their offices and jailhouse. Not that the jail offered much protection; it was only a rough stockade, located next door to the Buena Vista saloon.

Soon word spread, and the people from the road gathered in the Idaho City cemetery, only about a block from the courthouse. By most accounts, there were more than nine hundred of them, some of them members of the local vigilante organization based out of Payette. Mob mentality quickly took over. They were determined to lynch Patterson, and for several days they kept a vigil. The town's "fighting parson," Elder Kingsley, offered prayer for the success of the lynching.

On the second day they chose a leader. William McConnell, a future Idaho governor and senator, was the leader of the Payette vigilantes, and was well respected in the region. The mob asked him to take over. McConnell was sympathetic; Pinkham had been a friend of his (and McConnell, too, was a Union Republican). Reconnoitering the situation, he told the group, "We can take that jail." There was a roar in favor, but then he poured cold water on it: If they tried, he said, "It will be at

William McConnell, the well-respected leader of the Payette vigilantes
Courtesy Idaho State Historical Society

the cost of many lives. I cannot see the sense of sacrificing forty or fifty good men's lives for the purpose of hanging one murderer."

That seemed to end it, and as the group began to break up, McConnell started to ride out of the mountains. He was accompanied by Rube Robbins. Then a breathless horseman dashed up behind them with news. About a hundred of the most angry members of the mob had collected at Gilkie's smith shop, and the sheriff had approached them and ordered them to disperse. This only infuriated them. In minutes they had changed their minds and were planning to storm the courthouse. The sheriff in turn collected a crowd of a hundred or more—many of them Patterson's friends—and prepared for battle.

When McConnell and Robbins arrived, both sides were ready to shoot, and a single bullet would have begun an extended battle. McConnell moved out between the groups and negotiated a settlement.

Somehow the peace held, for month after month, until the trial in November. Newspapers across the West did their best to keep things inflamed, taking either Patterson's or Pinkham's side depending on their partisan leaning. The *Idaho World* in Idaho City was in Patterson's corner; the *Idaho Tri-Weekly Statesman* in Boise wanted him hanged.

The trial lasted six days, and testimony regarding many details of the shooting conflicted. The most skilled lawyer was defense attorney Frank Ganahl, who argued that Pinkham was simply waiting for a chance to shoot Patterson. One report said that "men and women alike were crying when Ganahl finished his impassioned plea."

It apparently worked. The jury was out for an hour and a half and returned with a verdict of "not guilty."

Calculating the odds for survival, Ferd Patterson split town as soon as he was released.

But he failed to calculate well enough.

Patterson fled west, to Walla Walla, pausing there to rest. We don't know where he was headed next, because his journey ended at a barber shop at Walla Walla. He was in the chair, his face under a hot towel prior to shaving, when another man entered the shop and pulled a gun.

It's been said that Patterson was fast enough on the draw to yank the towel from his head and actually pull his gun from the holster in the moments between the firing of the shots and his almost instant death from them. But the stories vary.

The way Ferd Patterson lived his life, he left open many possibilities for suspects: No lack of people wanted him dead.

Justice Overtaken

One day in the spring of 1865, the first piece of law enforcement intelligence ever recorded in Idaho fell into the hands of the first elected sheriff of Ada County, David C. Updyke. It was a list—a closely guarded list—of the members of a group of gunmen based north and west of Boise, men who had hidden their identities but not their loyalties: These were Updyke's bitterest enemies.

With haste, Updyke moved on the information. First, he swore out a batch of warrants, more than two dozen, alleging various crimes ample to slap the gang behind bars. Second, he sent word to his trusted deputies and some of their friends, between twelve and twenty men in all. Deputized, armed, and mounted on fleet horses, they would ride over the Boise foothills to the little settlement of Horseshoe Bend. Updyke sent advance word for more of his supporters to join him there. The united forces would ride west through the Payette River canyon, toward the farm settlement of Payette, where most of the gunmen lived.

Updyke and his posse planned to hit under cover of darkness; leaving Boise at about four in the afternoon, they rode north as planned.

But they were not the first out of town. Another group of horsemen sped west to Payette, to warn the gunmen before the sheriff arrived. Their reasons were better than they might have seemed.

In the small settlement of Boise, home to just a few hundred people in 1865, there were few secrets. It was no secret that David Updyke had been put into office by a group of new-to-the-area ranchers and businessmen who had in common a past allegiance with the outlaw Plummer Gang of Montana. It was further no secret that Updyke had either participated in or abetted a series of stage robberies, murders, and other crimes, before and since his election. And it was no secret that the gunmen he was setting off to kill—for he had no intention of ever bringing them to a trial—were the members of the Payette Vigilantes, the closest thing the area then had to enforcement of the law.

The vigilantes had harassed Updyke for months, keeping him off balance, and he and his network had been after their names for nearly as long. His plan was to arrest them under cover of his office, then shoot them for resisting arrest.

The information sieve spoiled his plans.

When Updyke's group reached Horseshoe Bend, he discovered that his troops there were gone; he had no way of knowing they had already been run off. Determined to rely on surprise, the sheriff and his posse made their way west, through the narrow, rocky Payette River valley, heading to the just-settled flat farm and ranch land beyond. But they were stumbling along in the dark through country they did not know well.

And the surprise was soon on them, when the vigilantes stopped the posse and surrounded them, with forces outnumbering Updyke's two to one.

That spring evening was the turning point in the fortunes of David Updyke, Ada County's criminal sheriff. It had been, for a while, a classic story of a young man headed west who makes good, or at least prospers.

Updyke's beginnings were prosperous. His roots ran back to the trading companies of Holland, and to the early Dutch settlements in New York; his family in upstate New York had accumulated substantial wealth. But David Updyke, born about 1830 in the Cayuga Lake area of western New York, was a troubled youth, early considered a black sheep and prone to falling in with a group of local rowdies. By his mid-twenties he was persuaded that an open landscape might suit him better. So in 1859 he headed west, taking a ship the long way around South America, landing in California.

There, for a time, he worked off his energies as a stage driver, a job he held for two years. He had arrived a decade too late to participate in the forty-niner gold rush, and his ambitions were not satisfied. In early

1863 he heard about a fabulous gold strike in a place called the Boise Basin (the territory was not yet called Idaho), and he headed north, gold pan in hand. He was early enough in the diggings to uncover a little gold and save a little money; after more than a year, he could report savings of about $1,500. In late 1864 he migrated south with his savings to the new town of Boise. But those savings were far from enough to enrich or satisfy this restless and ambitious man.

He found more satisfaction in a deal he soon was able to make.

Updyke invested his $1,500 in business in Boise. But to accumulate quickly the range of businesses he soon had—first a livery stable in the center of town, then a saloon, then part ownership of a ferry, then part of a ranch south of town—he needed more. He got it from a group of well-heeled men who had migrated south from the settlements around the north Idaho gold fields. Their inspiration, and possibly Updyke's as well, was Henry Plummer.

Plummer, one of the remarkable figures in Western history, had some odd parallels to the Ada County sheriff. Like Updyke, he was a northeasterner (Plummer was a native of Maine) who sailed around South America to make his fortune in California, and like Updyke, did well there for a while, ranching and serving to some acclaim as a marshal. Then he killed a man in a duel and was convicted of murder; he was released from the California prison at San Quentin only after pressure was applied to the governor. From there he fled to the new mining camp of Lewiston. His work as a marshal gave him a better reputation than many in the rough community, and for a while he got away with presenting himself as a respectable married businessman (the businesses being fronts, the "wife" a prostitute hired for appearance's sake). He fit in smoothly at first. But soon he assembled around him a collection of wanted men who formed a gang, robbing mines, stores, and stages. Within a year Plummer's violence in the Lewiston, Orofino, and Elk City area made Idaho too hot for him—the last straw was his shooting of a saloonkeeper. He fled to Montana, where he set up operations

33

anew. Many of his gang members remained in Idaho, and as the gold finds cooled in the north, they took themselves and their assets south to Boise. And there, before long, they found someone to take the role Plummer had played for them in Lewiston.

The gang members could hide horses and other goods at Updyke's livery, and when they needed to lie low they hid out at his ranch south of town. They sifted the gold dust through various businesses in town, especially Updyke's saloon. When Ada County was formed, the group was threatened with the arrival of law enforcement. But they solved that problem by electing Updyke as sheriff, along with several other friendly county officers.

Updyke, ever ready with a gun, sometimes joined them on their expeditions.

The best-known exploit was led by a man called Brockie Jack, an outlaw recently escaped from western Oregon and in hiding on one of the Boise area ranches. He dared to visit Updyke's saloon one day in May of 1865 to meet with the sheriff and two other gunmen, Willy Whittmore and Fred Williams. They were intrigued by a new stage line, not yet a year old, running from Montana to Utah through barely populated eastern Idaho. On the last day of the month, they rode east and camped near Fort Hall, at a place now called Ross Fork Creek. From there they dispatched Williams to Montana, to learn more about the gold shipments the stage carried and to ride as passengers on the stage they intended to rob.

The group was patient; the stage did not depart until late July, with seven passengers and an experienced driver. Five days into the trip, on July 26, it crossed Ross Fork Creek and then stopped, blocked by boulders that had been put in the road by the robbers. As soon as the stage stopped, the three robbers came into view.

One passenger, a gambler named Sam Martin, leaned out his window, saw what was happening, and yelled out. He pulled a revolver and, aiming at Whittmore, shot him in the hand. Whittmore, who was renowned for his short fuse, fired at the stage over and over, intending to shoot anyone inside, probably forgetting that one of his own accomplices was still in there. Williams was barely able to escape, though shot in the arm, along with the driver and one other passenger, all of whom ran off into the hills. But by the time Brockie Jack pulled the rifle from Whittmore's hands, the damage was done. To his horror, he saw that the five other passengers—including a Mormon couple on their way home to Utah—were lying still. One passenger was actually alive but acted dead to survive. The robbery had abruptly escalated to mass murder.

Brockie Jack called out, "My God. They're all dead."

Their horror didn't last long, nor did it slow their looting, once the thieves discovered that the stage held everything promised, including fifteen large gold bars, and bags of gold dust. The haul was estimated at $86,000—a fortune in the usual run of stage robberies. The robbers broke camp and sped back to Boise.

After they left, the stage driver, Charlie Parks, cautiously made his way back to the stage, where he and the one uninjured passenger made comfortable the one survivor, then headed off to the next stop on the stage route. He had a story to tell, because he had recognized both Brockie Jack and David Updyke, and quickly spread the word about how the new Ada County sheriff was moonlighting as a stage robber. The other living and mobile stage passenger had recognized the other two robbers. He was seconded by the stage company's insurer, which put a $10,000 reward on return of the gold and capture of the robbers.

The insurance company never retrieved its gold, which remains among the legendary unfound treasures of the West. The gold bars, which were marked and numbered, were never recorded as being sold, which usually would have been the case, nor was there a report of the gold dust matching the description of the stolen bags. Since none of the four robbers showed any signs of wealth when they were next seen, or ever again, the assumption since has been that they buried their treasure somewhere. But no one has ever learned where. One popular speculation has been the City of Rocks area, south of Albion, which would have been a distinctive location with prominent natural landmarks.

That summer Updyke remained sheriff of Ada County, and he still had strong local friends. But the confrontation with the Payette Vigilantes had not gone well, and strengthened the vigilantes' hand. The plotting to get rid of Updyke began in earnest. But driving out the crooked sheriff would not be easy.

First, in August 1865, only five months after the county's first election, the commissioners ordered and held another one. Several new county officials were elected, including the county's first district attorney. Updyke was ousted when the voters chose John Duvall, part owner of a ferry on the Boise River, as the new sheriff. But the change did not take effect immediately: Duvall's term did not start until the new year. In the meantime, Updyke still held the office.

As with Al Capone more than half a century later, they got him on bookkeeping. At that time the sheriff had the job of collecting taxes, and Updyke fulfilled that duty—but the taxes had a way of sticking to him, instead of being turned over to the county treasurer. As the treasurer and county commissioners noted the discrepancies between those who said they had paid and the lack of income, they focused on the sheriff.

In September the commissioners ordered the new district attorney, Albert Heed, to file charges against Updyke for misusing and embezzling county funds including the collected taxes, and for failing to arrest for murder West Jenkins, a quick-tempered member of Updyke's gang. Faced with confronting Updyke, Heed instead resigned. The commissioners, undeterred, appointed a new prosecutor and ordered him to file the charges. The commissioners then instructed sheriff-elect Duvall, who as yet had no official powers, to arrest Updyke.

The community held its collective breath at that point, but the new sheriff soon showed himself tougher than almost anyone had suspected. Collecting help from around town, he managed to arrest Updyke and lock him up in his own jail. A grand jury was then called to decide whether to file charges against him. Having done all that, Duvall and the members of the grand jury had to watch as Updyke coolly posted bond and returned to the other side of the jail bars, taking over his office once again.

Charges made their way to court anyway, and Updyke was notified he had to appear before a judge on October 5. On the day before he was to appear in court, he lost his nerve. Hoping to clear the books, he turned over to the treasurer all of the tax money he had collected, and resigned as sheriff. A deal may have been involved, because while the county officials got those concessions from Updyke, the deposed sheriff got something too: One of his own deputies, William West, and not Duvall, was named as interim sheriff through the end of the year.

But the ex-sheriff kept one step ahead of everyone else. In February 1866 word came to Boise of military troubles with one of the nearby Indian tribes. A group of volunteers, including some of the old gang members, was formed, and they elected Updyke as their captain. As they marched off toward the battle, and then back to Boise, the gang had a new front for its activities, and Updyke, his popularity partially restored, had fresh protection.

It didn't last long. In April, only weeks after the volunteers had returned home, a man who had sold horses to the group sued for non-payment. Updyke and his crew defied him. But one of Updyke's lieutenants, Reuben Raymond, was persuaded to testify that the volunteer outfit was little more than a cover for criminal activity. No sooner had he testified than another of Updyke's group, John Clark, hunted Raymond down and shot him to death. The new sheriff, Duvall, seized Clark and held him in the jail, about which Clark and Updyke couldn't much complain. Had Duvall not seized Clark, a mob in town, outraged by the Raymond shooting, would have hanged Clark.

Updyke made the situation worse, loudly proclaiming his threats about what he would do to the people of Boise if Clark wasn't released. At that point, sympathy for him vanished, and groups of armed men took to patrolling the streets. Updyke and his men went into hiding, and even Duvall apparently decided he could do little more. Clark was next seen dead, hanging from a gibbet constructed under cover of night, on the site of what is now the Idaho State Capitol.

Updyke's first reaction was to redouble his threats. Then, worried about what Clark might have said as he faced death, and realizing his remaining allies were few, he collected one of his last friends, Jake Dixon, and fled Boise.

He headed into the mountains northeast of town on April 12, veering away from the Boise Basin gold fields where he was still well known, off into the deeper recesses of still newer mining fields, on the rough road to Rocky Bar on the west side of the Sawtooth Mountains. It was some of the highest and most rugged country in the West. That night, Updyke and Dixon found a deserted cabin near Syrup Creek to rest.

They evidently didn't know they were being followed by members of the Payette Vigilantes. The vigilantes tracked them to the cabin and surprised them. Under cover of darkness they marched Updyke and Dixon to a shed near Syrup Creek where they stopped and questioned Updyke. The former sheriff is said to have refused to say a word.

It was his last choice. The next day, he and Dixon were found swinging from nooses in the remote shed.

After his rich history of robbing, thieving, and conniving, Updyke is said to have died with fifty dollars in his pockets.

The Storyteller

Henry McDonald knew George Myers from the hauling business, though not well. Based on what he did know, he thought that in Myers he could see his own future. He had no notion that he was also seeing the end of his future.

McDonald was a piecework hauler in the Wood River Valley, carrying supplies from one town to another in the still-booming mining district, usually accompanied only by his dog. He occasionally veered south, out of that valley, over some low hills and into the Snake River plain. There he would bump into an older and better-used trail, between the Boise and Boise Basin settlements to the west and the Salt Lake City area to the southeast. Haulers took that road often as the best way to get from one set of settlements to the other; there were none to speak of in between.

McDonald had some ambition. He wanted to buy an outfit—horses, a wagon, the equipment he needed to haul longer distances running his own business; he'd had it with being a wage slave. He put out the word on the road, when he ran into other haulers, that he was interested in buying, though he was unclear about how much money he had to spend. After a few months, a reply came back to him. George Myers, a veteran of the trade, was looking to cash out. Communications, slow but direct for the era, were sent out. McDonald wanted to buy, Myers was willing to sell. Across the sagebrush desert routes, secondhand and thirdhand word went about that a business deal seemed to be in the works.

The two arranged to meet at a spot called Soul's Rest, on the Boise–Salt Lake trail. McDonald joined Myers on his run, hired on to begin with as an employee, with the idea of taking over before long, bringing his dog along for the ride. The two of them headed west through the desert south of Hailey. It was not an especially rigorous journey. But in the days ahead, they got no rest.

A man in over his depth: Henry McDonald

Myers was a cranky old man, a heavy drinker—and he was drinking on this trip—efficient enough at his business but not especially likable. McDonald was utterly unfamiliar with the realities of business, especially of buying or selling one. We don't know exactly for how much Myers was willing to sell his established operation with an established clientele, but a figure around $2,000 to $3,000, or maybe more, seems likely.

McDonald had nowhere near that kind of money. He had little more than pocket change. He was hoping he could pay Myers over time. The negotiations fell apart quickly and that set the tone for their relationship. The arguments were only the beginning.

They argued about everything. When in early September a group of freighters passed them, they overheard Myers and McDonald yelling at each other about McDonald's dog, which kept falling out of the wagon. Myers threatened to shoot the dog, McDonald would recall later.

The exact circumstances of Myers's death were never made clear. He and McDonald probably came to blows, and Myers fell to the ground and was run over by the wagon—either accidentally or on purpose. That much would at least be consistent with the facts police eventually unearthed.

The truth has been buried in the almost impenetrable web of lies McDonald began telling as soon as he encountered the next road traveler—and picked up as soon as he hit town.

Today the word "teamster" is associated with the international labor union, but decades ago, and in the old West, it had a different meaning, implicit in the word itself. A teamster was the driver of a team—sometimes of a mule train, sometimes of a half-dozen oxen, or sometimes several horses. In conversation at the time, any of these would usually be called an "outfit."

Henry McDonald, who drove teams for the purpose of delivering supplies between the mines of Utah and Idaho, was a teamster for hire; he did not own his own outfit. His desire to become an independent businessman was what led him to the gallows and resulted in the only legal execution in Idaho's most rugged area and still among its most lightly populated, Owyhee County.

The few surviving pictures of McDonald suggest a wiry man, tall, thin, with a thick, bushy mustache, but by frontier standards, carefully groomed. He gave off no sense of the hardened desperado. But the look in his eyes is a bit like those of a deer in the headlights, a man perpetually caught by surprise with the reality around him and never quite able to catch up. Although his job of driving teams from one town to another would not seem especially stressful, apart from the normal hazards of the road, he often seemed a man in over his depth.

We do not know much about McDonald's early life. As much as he liked to talk and write, he never had much to say about his early years—not that we would necessarily believe him if he had. Probably, he emigrated from an eastern or southern state in the 1870s, looking for work in the western mines. As of 1880, when he was driving teams between Kelton, Utah, and the Idaho mines in the Wood River Valley and in the Silver City area, he said that his mother was still alive and he had a wife and two children. He gave the impression that they were still living in the Salt Lake City area, just south of Kelton, but few Idahoans ever heard much more about them than that, and Henry McDonald spoke of them only toward the very end of his life, when he was facing the death penalty.

In the summer of 1880 he quit his job hauling goods around the Wood River area to pick up on a new opportunity. He hired on with George Myers, a long-timer on the Utah–Idaho route who owned an outfit and was said to be interested in selling out. They both told people in Idaho that McDonald planned to buy, and at Soul's Rest, McDonald joined the haul with Myers.

One day in September McDonald showed up in Boise with a load and the outfit, pulling through that place on his way to Silver City. Freighters familiar with everyone's horses and wagons—they were distinctive identifiers—noticed that while Myers's outfit was pulling into town, someone else was driving it, and Myers was nowhere around.

McDonald stopped only briefly in Boise; he had a load bound for the Silver City mining district. But the questions and concerns were enough to prompt the Ada County sheriff, Joe Oldham, to mount up, ride out of town, and catch up with him on the route. Somewhere out in the desert flats near the town of Mayfield, he stopped McDonald and began to ask questions.

"These are Myers's wagon and horses," the sheriff said. "Where is Myers?"

McDonald said they weren't Myers's any more, that he had sold him the outfit for $600 down, which he had paid, and $800 in regular payments to be paid later. After they had concluded their business out on the trail, he said, Myers had taken off.

Oldham pressed him. "Where did Myers go?"

"Oh, I remember now," Myers said. "There had been a horse Myers had lost in the war with the Bannock Indians, and someone we passed told him he had heard it was spotted somewhere in Oregon. And then Myers rode off to try to find it."

The sheriff found none of this very convincing. McDonald had admitted wanting Myers's outfit and he didn't look to Oldham like the sort to be able to buy it outright, or even with $600 down—he didn't seem the type who was able to put that much money together in one place at one time. Figuring McDonald for a liar, Oldham hauled him back to Boise and jailed him at the courthouse while he pondered a search for the body. McDonald insisted that wasn't necessary. I'll be proven innocent, he insisted. You'll see the evidence. Before the pair had split up, he said, Myers had posted a letter to the Boise area that would prove McDonald's innocence.

But Sheriff Oldham held him behind bars. Then, several weeks later, William Morlatt, a freighter on the road to Idaho City, dropped by the sheriff's office with a letter bearing the signature of George Myers, dated in October, quite a while after McDonald had been jailed. Addressed to Morlatt, it advised him, "I have sold me team too Henry McDonald, and have got track of that horse of mine and am going to find him."

It sounded just like the letter McDonald had told the sheriff to expect. Maybe a little too much like it.

There was just one problem, Morlatt said. He'd gotten letters from Myers before, had done business with the man, and he knew his signature. And this wasn't it.

The sheriff discussed the situation with Tom Calahan, the prosecutor. Avoiding any mention of the letter, Calahan grilled McDonald, who repeated that a letter should be coming. Calahan said he didn't believe it. McDonald told him that Myers must have been held up by robbers on the road. The lonesome trails were dangerous places, after all.

McDonald's comments probably did spark a new line of inquiry, though, among the people at stage stops and out on the road. Sheriff Oldham and territorial officials sent out inquires, and got some responses. They found a group of freighters who remembered seeing Myers and McDonald together in early September, and not getting along well: Apparently they had been arguing about McDonald's dog. At another stop, one of them heard a new story from McDonald, who was traveling alone now. According to this story, their arguments had gotten worse, Myers had reached for a gun but slipped under a wagon wheel, and was badly injured, with bones broken. McDonald said he was trying to fix his wounds when three other riders, apparently immigrants from a European country, appeared and said they would take care of Myers, so McDonald rode off.

McDonald was held in jail for an appearance before the grand jury.

Oldham and Calahan were frustrated. The case was far from airtight, and they knew it. McDonald was obviously a liar, but they had no body and no solid evidence—only possibilities. They knew they needed more, so they tried a trick.

Bill Glines, a short-time offender, was installed in the cell next to McDonald's. Unlike McDonald, he had some education, and since McDonald was only marginally literate, he called Glines over and asked for help in writing a few letters.

Glines did, not writing them personally but holding a candle and advising McDonald on how to write and improve his grammar and spelling.

The main cover letter, addressed to a bartender friend at Kelton, Utah, said this:

"Dear George, I am in a tite place. If I have to stay for the grand jury I am gone for good. Now doo mee a favor, for this does depend on my life and I will make it all rite with you when I see you. George, be sure and see some of Myers hand rite and sine his name as near like it as you can. George now dont fail and don't write anything but the affair between me and Myers because the sheriff opens letters and reads them."

The inmates also wrote a couple of enclosures, letters dated in November that purported to be from Myers and addressed to McDonald—suggesting he was still alive.

As soon as they were done, Glines grabbed the letters and handed them over to the sheriff, to McDonald's roaring fury. Prosecutors now had another lie on record, and samples of McDonald's handwriting to match the earlier letters, but they still had no body.

However, a man named Lewis, related to another occasional teamster named Len Lewis, was traveling near what is now Glenns Ferry when he noticed clothes, boots, and rope off the trail. Looking more closely, he found bones. There was no certain identification, but it all fit the description of George Myers.

The location was believed to be in Owyhee County, so the sheriff and prosecutor moved their prisoner to Silver City, the county seat. McDonald had tried to tunnel his way out of the Ada County jail, an effort that failed early, but he soon saw he had no hope at Silver City. There, the cells were built into a cave on the mountainside.

By the time of his trial in the spring of 1881, McDonald had said that Myers had lit out for Oregon, that he had been killed by robbers, that he had been injured on the road and hauled off by travelers, even—in his last letters—that he had taken ill. At his trial, he took the witness stand, and delivered what he said was the real, complete story. It could not have been told before, he said, because he feared for his life from two other men.

He said that he had heard Myers wanted to sell his outfit, and he—McDonald—wanted to buy. He hopped another wagon headed for Kelton, the same direction Myers was taking, and caught up with him. They agreed to the sale of the outfit, he said, and signed papers to that effect at Salmon Falls, south of present-day Twin Falls.

Myers was not, McDonald said, an easy traveling companion. He drank heavily and turned into a mean drunk, berating McDonald and abusing his dog. Finally, as they were riding back through southern Idaho, they argued about the dog and Myers reached for his pistol in the wagon's jockey box, saying he was going to shoot the dog. Instead, he fell out of the wagon and slipped under one of the axles, and then a wheel ran over part of his body. The horses kept on and the wagon dragged him a few feet before McDonald could get full control and grind the outfit to a halt.

He was struggling to pull Myers, who was probably already dead, out from under the wagon, he said, when two men, Len Lewis—the uncle of the man who had found Myers's body—and Frank Kellet, rode by. They pulled Myers's body to the side, but they would not help him load it for the trip to Salmon Falls, the nearest community. As McDonald explained it, they had been looking for a crime to blame on a man named Gus Glenn, and they would set up the evidence to frame him. And, McDonald said, they warned him on pain of death to say nothing about the plot.

And, he suggested, that explains how it was that Lewis's nephew was the finder of Myers's body.

It was McDonald's first detailed story, and it caused a big stir. It established his creativity, at least, since it seemed on the surface to tie up most of the loose ends in his many earlier stories.

But the prosecution was well prepared, as usual. Territorial officials had located Len Lewis and established that he was hundreds of miles away from Idaho when the incident occurred. Kellet was never found, and McDonald was unable to find anyone who would say they even knew him, including Lewis. Nor could anyone find out anything about the mysterious Glenn.

The jury concluded McDonald was lying again and he was sentenced to hang in August. The event was delayed for two months with appeals to the territorial Supreme Court. But it would not be delayed long: The court set a hanging date in October.

On that day, McDonald was escorted in a wagon from his cave jail to the nearby mining town of Ruby City, then out beyond that small town to a cemetery where the gallows had been constructed. Though the day was overcast and, by the time of the hanging, raining as well, hundreds of people showed up to watch—McDonald had been big news across Idaho for months.

The man who had told so many stories that didn't pan out, however, did get it right in his last reported statement. A few miles out from the place of execution, seeing some people hurrying along beside the wagon carrying him to the gallows, McDonald is said to have remarked:

"Take your time. There won't be much going on before I get there."

Counterfeit

From a distance, Jim and Lewis Eddy looked alert and cheerful as they rode up the trail along Shingle Creek, past the small herd of cattle their families owned. The assorted Eddys and Splawns, members of the two families living creekside in this fold under the Seven Devils Mountains, peered out from the Eddy house into the brisk late fall day, and figured that for a good sign. The meeting at Weiser with Emmett Taylor must have gone well. It meant the work they had been preparing for could begin.

Had anyone in Weiser taken note, the sight of the two backwoodsmen meeting with Taylor, a respected professional in town, must have seemed a little odd. But there's no record anyone noticed, and the Eddys casually rode off with the package from Chicago. They did not stop often on the road north, and only small communities lay between Weiser and their home anyway. Pollock was the closest, and it was ten or more miles away.

As they rode up to the house, checked the doors, and double-checked to make sure the family members on guard up and down the creek were in their places, they pulled out their supplies. Their supplies did not consist of food and sundries from town, but of manufacturing equipment. As everyone watched, they opened a box and pulled out the wooden mold pieces: one matching the shape of a five-dollar gold piece, another a ten-dollar gold piece, the third a twenty-dollar piece. And there were near-duplicate wooden pieces, also needed for the work ahead.

Over the next couple of days, they assembled their materials and were ready to produce U.S. gold pieces—or at least reasonable facsimiles thereof. They decided to put in another order for more wooden molds immediately, as they would be needing them soon.

John Eddy and his family
Courtesy Idaho State Historical Society

They carefully poured plaster into a set of molds. Most plaster took a long time to dry and cure; limestone plaster could take a month, which would have made it worthless. But this was a special mix developed through their research and it cured almost immediately. Once the pieces were set, they were taken to a kiln out back and fired there.

Now they were ready for metal application, which had three steps.

The plaster pieces were put inside another set of molds, which had small openings on the sides. The Eddys and Splawns melted down a batch of metals—tin, copper, and lead—into an alloy, and then poured it thinly over the plaster. The layer was so thin that the coins' design remained sharp, but the alloy was strong enough to withstand wear, at least for a while.

The last step was the trickiest. The coins had to look as if they were made of solid gold, and the counterfeiters had prepared a liquid mix with a small amount of gold, together with other metals and chemicals, to create that impression. The surface had to be durable enough that the gold sheen wouldn't wear away too fast. This meant the backcountry families had to use a method that was high-tech for the 1880s. They acquired a large electric battery, able to supply a substantial current—this too had taken some research and effort. The coins were then placed in a tub with metal salts and other components, and a jolt of electric current from the battery was applied.

Not long after, the Splawns and Eddys were looking at their new pile of bright and shiny five-, ten-, and twenty-dollar gold pieces. They may have had plaster hearts, but on quick inspection they looked real, and they looked all the more real after the Splawns and Eddys jostled them around, to test their wear and give them a well-used look.

The whole process took a few weeks, and a few months later the metallic odors and smoke in the little valley were long gone, cleared away by wind and rain. The stack of coins sitting in the Eddy house was their little secret.

Now all they had to do was spend them.

Where the Splawns and Eddys came from before Idaho isn't clear, and neither is whether they had a close relationship before their arrival in the Rapid River basin. They do seem to have had some earlier experience as cowboys or cattlemen.

They arrived quietly in 1886, and little notice was taken at first. Not many people lived then in the Little Salmon River country, only a few in Pollock, south of the Rapid. There were few people several miles to the north of Riggins, which had been first settled in 1863 by men who thought they had spotted some flecks of gold at the confluence of the Salmon and the Little Salmon. There was no gold rush in the area—though there had been to the northeast, in Florence—but every so often, someone came to the area hoping for a find. The Splawns and Eddys, to judge from their later history, may have been among them, looking for gold in the unpopulated creeks off Rapid River. The Eddys settled on Shingle Creek, off the Rapid, and the Splawns a few miles north of them on Papoose Creek.

To the outside world they appeared to be small-scale farmers and cattlemen. They didn't interact much with the few neighbors who did live in the area, and the cattle they had weren't purchased locally. They seem to have had generally self-sufficient lives in the backcountry for their first few years there.

They were tight families, as close as any. They lived together and worked together, did not fly off in different directions, and were intensely loyal. As many of them as there were, there was never a question of dividing them or turning one against the rest.

Then something gave them some ambition. We don't know what the precise motivation was, but it seems to have involved a combination of factors. The early 1890s were a time of excitement in the Seven Devils. Big finds of copper and smaller discoveries of precious metals were located, mining began on a big scale, and a good deal of ore money began to float around the area.

To the north, beyond Riggins, White Bird, and Grangeville, the Nez

Perce Indian Reservation was opened for settlement by non-tribal members. That meant the tribes were suddenly receiving money for land from the white settlers; conservative in finance, they preferred gold coins rather than paper money for their payments. In all directions money was changing hands on a regular basis.

Maybe, too, after most of a decade scratching by, the Eddys and Splawns were simply getting tired of the way things had been and were growing weary of livestock. The Eddys had a history as horsemen, as alongside the cattle they raised horses. They especially loved horse racing—an urban endeavor, engaged in informally in many places around Idaho but especially popular at Lewiston.

At first the families decided to counterfeit gold coins for use at the horse races, in Lewiston and other tracks around the northwest. The technical details eluded them at first, but during a visit to Weiser members of the family met a well-educated local man named Emmett Taylor, who bought into the scheme and helped them devise their manufacturing operation.

The families began using the coins, and they were accepted routinely at the Lewiston track and other locations. For several years they traveled around the region and often exchanged the coins for paper cash. Money exchanged quickly and easily at the track, and once passed it was hard to track. They also exchanged money at county fairs—six of the group managed to work fairs around the region—and other big events, wherever they could easily blend into the crowd. Besides, the families must have figured, counterfeiting was usually assumed to be an urban crime, especially counterfeiting involving the minting of coins. Rapid River was not a suspect town for an illicit mint.

They also made sure never to spend any of their homemade money near Riggins or Grangeville. The spending and exchanging had to be farther afield. That way, they assumed, even if the coins were uncovered as fake, they'd never be caught.

Charley Reavis, a clerk in a Salt Lake City hardware store, was a young man with motivation. In the 1890s the profession of detective had just come into national prominence, and Reavis overflowed with ambition. Just graduated from high school, he wanted to take a course in detection, if he could find one. But the opportunities in Salt Lake seemed slim. He had no immediate path to get himself from store clerk to polished detective, but one day the unlikely opportunity opened to him as he worked in the store.

A man who seemed to be unfamiliar with Salt Lake, and had a back-country manner about him, had walked into the store, looking for a box of nails, an item available for only a few cents. Reavis collected the box. The man apologized and said he had only a twenty-dollar gold piece to pay for it. Reavis opened the cash drawer and made change for the twenty, handing back nearly that much to the customer, along with the nails. The man thanked him and walked out.

Something about the exchange struck Reavis as peculiar—a back-country man with only a large-denomination coin available, to pay for an item costing a few cents? He strolled from behind the counter and over to the front window, and looked down the street. He saw the man casually walking along and then, a block or so away, he saw him toss the box of nails into an alley.

Reavis saw his opportunity and ran with it.

He took the coin to federal officials in Salt Lake, where they quickly determined it was a fake. Then they told Reavis something else: A big reward, a thousand dollars from the U.S. Department of the Treasury, was waiting for anyone who could help federal authorities bring in the counterfeiters. Reavis was highly interested—he already knew what one of them looked like. Reavis soon learned that the investigation was being run out of Lewiston, Idaho, where the largest number of bad coins had been found. Reavis made his way there.

The U.S. marshal at Lewiston, Eben Mounce, had not been sitting quietly amid the counterfeiting. He knew the horse tracks, especially the

Lewiston horse races, were the main distribution points for the bad coins. He and his men quietly interviewed people around the tracks, trying to get a sense of the money flow. Gradually the prime suspects began to emerge: the Eddy and Splawn families. One or another of the family members always seemed to be around when the bad gold coins appeared. And while people could recall them handing them out, no one could recall their taking one.

The research into the families continued, and what the law learned matched with the passage of bad money. The families traveled a lot, and they seemed to spend more than they ought to have been able to afford. But although they were good suspects, there was no proof. The hideaway off the Rapid River was well guarded, and any attempt to storm the place would fail before it began. No one knew when the gold pieces were made, or how, or where the incriminating evidence might be. There always seemed to be family members in the area to stop anyone who ventured near. Even getting through at all with anything short of a small army seemed to be unlikely.

Reavis knew another route needed to be taken. His route would begin at the horse track. Reavis searched around for the fastest horse he could find that hadn't already become visible on the track. Reavis finally located a mare named Nancy Hanks, a little horse that was nonetheless very fast. He entered her in the Lewiston races, opposite a couple of Jim Eddy's horses. Nancy Hanks beat Eddy's horses.

Reavis made a point of introducing himself to Jim Eddy, and of making sure that what started as a competition developed into a friendship.

The amateur detective told parts of the truth. He had no good source of income, he said, and Nancy Hanks was his only big asset. As he met the Eddys and the Splawns a second time, and a third, he suggested that he was nearing destitution, looking for some kind of an opportunity.

They asked him whether he would be willing to part with Nancy Hanks. The answer was no, because she was his main opportunity. But he suggested maybe a half-interest, in return for some other enterprise that might also, on some level, be a moneymaker.

The Eddys and Splawns talked it over. The kid—still not much more than a teenager, certainly presented as no kind of law enforcement official—seemed to be on the level. They had never let an outsider into the family business before, but, well, this looked like an unusual case. Nancy Hanks was a special horse, and they wanted her. Their recent prosperity had eaten away at their long-running discipline, and started to infect it with the idea that whatever they really wanted, they could have because they could afford it.

Jim Eddy sent a message north to Lewiston inviting William Reavis down to the Rapid River. Reavis jumped at the opportunity. He took a stage south to Grangeville, met there with Mounce to tell him what he was up to, and then headed into the wilderness, up the Rapid River, and into the compound of two families having an unaccustomed internal battle.

Jim Eddy, the group's most fanatic horse watcher, had extended the invitation to Reavis without telling the others. The family had managed its operations successfully so far by letting no one else inside except for Emmett Taylor, and he had been a necessity. Domestically the Eddys and Splawns may not have taken kindly to this outside partner.

Once Reavis was there, however, they had a problem. He had told people where he was going, and if he simply disappeared there might be trouble. And besides that, Jim Eddy was fiercely determined to have Nancy Hanks, whom Reavis had left behind in Lewiston. The families finally concluded that he could stay, and they would observe him and make their decision when they felt comfortable with it. So for the next three months, Reavis spent his time at the Eddy and Splawn houses, helping with the chores. The families did not let him actually witness the counterfeiting. But he learned a good deal about it anyway, and he persuaded them over time that he might be able to pass some of the coins himself, over in Oregon, where he was unknown.

After three months, the families' attitudes eased, and they decided Reavis could be trusted. They effectively let him into the family, explained the operation to him, and put the offer to him: half of Nancy Hanks for a slice of the counterfeiting revenues. Reavis eagerly accepted.

He helped the families where he could. He also learned where the supplies were kept, where the molds and dies were located—some of them buried in the yard—and where the coins were stashed before being taken into town.

Over time, Reavis came and went between Rapid River and Lewiston. Watching his tracks closely, he stayed in touch with Mounce, and the two of them worked with the Idaho County sheriff, W. M. Williams. Eventually they hatched a plan to finally nail the counterfeiters.

It would go down during the sale of a nearby cattle ranch, owned by the Allison family. A story was concocted that cattle were missing, and Williams issued a warrant for the arrest of Jim Eddy, on a charge of cattle theft. When two members of the families showed up in Grangeville, they were arrested and jailed at the county courthouse at Mount Idaho.

Reavis made his way back down to Rapid River, and told the tale: The charges were thin and could be beaten, but it would take a show of force to do it. Everyone the family could muster should show up in that courthouse at Jim Eddy's arraignment. Together, they could provide the evidence and the force to get this legal problem quashed. Otherwise, he warned, the prosecution likely would continue.

They accepted his advice, and one morning in 1986 the rest of the two families, except for Ike Splawn who was at Lewiston, set off for Mount Idaho. When they arrived in the courtroom, the doors were shut behind them, and all were arrested. The charges: counterfeiting gold coins.

The Eddy women were soon free, however, and they returned to Rapid River. Reavis showed up, and with his help they buried all the evidence—all the equipment, machinery, molds, and metals. They did not yet know Reavis was undercover, but they soon would.

At the trial in May of 1897 at the federal courthouse in Moscow, Reavis took the stand and told how he had infiltrated the clans and how the operation worked. The equipment and supplies for counterfeiting were all produced; Reavis had helped the federal agents who went searching and unearthed what the sisters had buried.

The trial lasted six days and the jury was sent out for supper, returned, and within a couple of hours had verdicts. They found Jim Eddy guilty on all eight counts, John Eddy guilty on all eight counts, Emmett Taylor guilty on six counts, Charles Scroggin guilty on four counts, Ike Splawn guilty on four counts, and Stan Splawn and Newt Eddy guilty of conspiracy, and two minors were "recommended to the mercy of the court."

Jim and John Eddy and Emmett Taylor were sentenced to sixteen years of hard labor. The rest received lighter sentences.

The few Eddys who remained out of prison eventually sold off the property at Shingle Creek, and were said to have left for Oregon.

The fake gold coins seem to have disappeared from sight. None of them seems to have surfaced in recent years.

Nancy Hanks, the horse whose speed was used to bring down the families, was poisoned at Meadows, while Reavis was testifying the case at Moscow.

And Reavis?

A few accounts float around as to the rest of life. According to one story, he was beaten to death near Culdesac; in another version he was fatally shot; and a third says he lived out his life near Enterprise, Oregon, where he ran a livery stable.

Just possibly, Reavis had had enough excitement for one lifetime.

Diamondfield Jack

Out on the south Cassia County hills, in the land claimed as grazing territory by the cattlemen, where the sheepmen grazed their flocks and visitors were few, the sight of a new face was welcome, even though some new faces meant trouble.

Not long past daybreak on the morning of February 4, 1886, two young Mormon sheep tenders, Daniel Cummings and John Wilson, saw a horseman riding their way. Although they were in the middle of fixing breakfast, they were glad to see him. He was Davis Hunter, another sheepman whose flock was also located in the no man's land, a few miles to the west. He was pulling a two-wheeled cart, and unloaded for Cummings and Wilson a small stack of firewood he had chopped. He and the cart were headed to the small town of Oakley, about thirty miles away, to pick up supplies.

All seemed well at the camp. The sheep were nearby, under close observation, close enough that the two sheepdogs were still tied to a wheel of their wagon, not yet needed to rein in the stragglers. The camp was neatly kept, and supplies were adequate. Their wagon, a supply carrier that doubled as a makeshift bunkhouse under a canvas cover, was in good shape.

As he rode off, Hunter was pleased to see things going so well, especially in a time of tension and some risk from the cattlemen. For the sheepmen had all been warned: Work this territory at the risk of death. All of the sheepmen were armed for protection from predators; but now the wolves and coyotes were the least of their fears.

And no one had warned them more often than a talkative, tough man named "Diamondfield" Jack Davis, a gunman for the Sparks-Harrell ranch, which stretched from Cassia County, Idaho, deep into Nevada. Of all the cattlemen and all their hired guns, Davis was the man they

The legendary "Diamondfield" Jack Davis
Courtesy Idaho State Historical Society

feared the most. He had actually shot a man some months before, and word of his heinous reputation spread fast in Cassia County.

A couple of days after Davis Hunter's visit, two other men rode up to Cummings and Wilson's camp. One of them was Jim Bower, the general manager of the immense Sparks-Harrell cattle ranch. The other was a friend of his, Jeff Gray.

The encounter started tensely, with a series of warnings blasting back and forth. Bower warned the sheepmen to stay out of cattle territory; the sheepmen said they would graze where they liked. The cattlemen moved in closer. The two angry sides were only a couple of feet apart.

Exactly what caused Gray, who must have been a quick shot, to fire his weapon is unknown. But evidence does suggest that, since he was closer to Wilson, he shot him first, a clean shot to the head, the bullet smashing through Wilson's chin into his brain. He crumpled to the ground. The shooter turned and fired at Cummings, hitting him in the stomach; he too fell in front of the wagon. Gray later said his shots were in self-defense; whether one of the sheepmen was brandishing a rifle, which was later found inside their wagon, remains a mystery.

Bower and Gray dragged the injured men inside the wagon, to keep them out of sight. They threw Wilson, who was barely alive but would not last long, onto the upper bed, and dragged Cummings to the foot of the bunk. The sheepmen's rifle was there, along with supplies and a few bullets for ammunition; Bower and Gray took nothing. In the commotion and in his haste to leave the scene, Gray dropped his corncob pipe.

Wilson died, never regaining consciousness, within a couple of hours. Cummings's end was more protracted and painful—he died a slow, drawn-out death, taking several hours to leave this earth.

The sheepdogs, tied to the wagon wheel, were left alone. They had water but no food, and after a few days they began to starve.

About a week later another sheepherder named Edgar Severe was walking around the hills and saw scattered sheep to the southeast, in the direction of Cummings and Wilson's camp. He rounded some of them up and headed for the camp. When he discovered what had happened there, he released the nearly dead sheepdogs, returned to his camp, and sent for one of the other herders. He sent a fast horseman named Noel Carlson to race to Oakley. From there, another rider and the sheriff were dispatched.

The investigation was haphazard. The scene was trampled not only by law enforcement but by curious sheepmen and cattlemen, and pieces of evidence such as bullets and clothing were passed around from person to person before the court got hold of them. The poor handling of the crime scene mattered little, because no one had any doubt that the killer was Diamondfield Jack.

Diamondfield's origins are unclear; he was sometimes said to have been born in Lynchburg, Virginia, sometime around 1870, though a search for birth records there came up empty. Moving west, he started as a typical knockabout, moving from this job to that, distinguished mostly by a tendency to brag and exaggerate. He tried mining for a while in Nevada, and his claims of what he found there led to the dubious nickname "Diamondfield."

By the early 1890s much of the rangeland in the northern interior West had been staked out by cattlemen who had arrived early enough to stake claim. In the early 1890s overgrazing and fierce winters degraded the pastureland for cattle feeding purposes. Owners of large flocks of sheep, which needed to roam and could happily graze on poor rangeland, began to move in. The two industries had an uneasy coexistence, to say the least. They loosely agreed, in the Cassia County area, that the cattlemen would stay generally west of Oakley.

But irritating incidents kept happening. The cattlemen took the conflict to a higher level. They hired gunmen to ride the ranges, to chase the sheep operators off what they considered to be their land. Their intent was mostly to intimidate. They told the gunmen to try to avoid shooting, but if need be, shoot to wound. If it turned into a matter of shooting to kill, well, the cattlemen would stand behind their guns.

Despite a lack of practical experience, Diamondfield Jack talked himself into one of these jobs, hired by the enormous Sparks-Harrell ranch in Cassia County. The pay was good, but his employers demanded results: The sheepmen had to be genuinely held back. Jack's region-wide reputation as a braggart didn't help much at first.

For a while, he simply talked big. He spread the word he was on "fighting wages." Encountering one pair of apparent sheepherders, he warned, "If the sheep come any farther, you'll be facing the muzzle of a Winchester."

The sheepmen were of split mind about Diamondfield. On one hand, he was a known braggart; on the other, some of his talk seemed so blood-thirsty that he might in fact be dangerous. One cold November day in 1895, a herder named Bill Tolman decided to call Jack's bluff. He found out where Jack was—at a shack on the Sparks-Harrell operation, in the Shoshone Valley—and rode up to it, his shotgun at the ready. A small crowd of sheepmen hung back, watching from a hill a quarter-mile away. He called out Jack, who emerged from the shed, his own gun at his side.

They talked, and then argued, for tense minutes and then an hour or more. Finally Jack Davis, either tiring of the debate or thinking that Tolman's patience was nearly ended, pulled his gun and fired, hitting Tolman in the shoulder. Tolman cried out in pain and dropped his own gun.

For all his rough talk, Jack Davis was no cold-blooded killer. A little startled by what he'd just done, he brought bandage material and water out of the shack to try to help Tolman. He called out to the sheepmen on the hill, telling them to collect their friend. None of them wanted to approach. So Davis, Tolman leaning on him, walked up to them and handed off the wounded man. Then he turned around and went back into the shack.

Once out of sight, Diamondfield Jack's bravado disappeared. He knew he was in trouble. For one thing, Tolman might die, and he might be arrested for murder. Even if Tolman recovered, the shooting might lead to trouble. A lot of law enforcement and a good portion of the politicians in southern Idaho sympathized more with the sheepmen than with the cattlemen, and the idea of taking out the most notorious cattle gunman of the day would be irresistible.

Jack Davis stopped in at Sparks-Harrell headquarters to collect his pay and to resign. He rode south to the nearest border, into Nevada. He spent several weeks at Wells, at the saloons and bordellos there. He ventured out a little further after the turn of the year, but he stayed mostly on the southern side of the Nevada-Idaho line, mainly hanging around the Middlestacks ranch, which was part of the Sparks-Harrell operation, carousing with the cowboys there.

One day in late January while he was staying there, Jack Davis rode off with another sometime gunman named Fred Gleason, to look for two horses that had wandered off. The search took them into Idaho sheep country. That night, wandering around in the dark, they unexpectedly rode up to a sheep camp. Startled, Davis reached for his gun quickly, almost as a reflex; but his horse startled, too, and Davis's finger accidentally pulled the trigger, and he shot into the ground. The sheepmen in the camp, alerted to the presence of two unexpected horsemen and probably quickly registering that Diamondfield Jack was one of them, grabbed their rifles and began to fire.

Maybe it was that no one was prepared and therefore shooting well, or maybe it was the darkness, but no people were hit by the dozen or so bullets that flew back and forth in the next few minutes. But Diamondfield Jack had added another shooting incident to his resume.

The shooting of the Mormon sheepherders, Cummings and Wilson, occurred about a week later. Around that time, Jack Davis was working around the Middlestacks, then said he was leaving there. He headed back south into Nevada, passed through Wells, then wound up in a string of ranches to its southwest, in the Lamoille Valley. There he regaled anyone who would listen with tales of his exploits, usually exaggerated—the sheepmen he had shot, the nighttime shooting at the sheep camp, and much more, real or imagined.

J. B. Green, who ran a general store in the valley, recalled later how a drunken Diamondfield Jack had wandered into his store, telling anyone who would listen about the sheepmen he had shot. That, as it turned out, was only shortly after news of the Cummings and Wilson murders had made its way there. People around northern Nevada and southern Idaho were beginning to put the pieces together.

Davis himself had heard nothing of the killings—yet.

He swung north again, drifting through the Middlestacks area again, and finally chanced into the news about Wilson and Cummings, and the realization that he was the prime suspect. After a little discussion with some of the ranchers and hired hands seeking advice on how to leave the country, he then switched course and rode hard south, through Nevada and into Arizona. He appeared to be headed to Mexico. Davis covered the desert, and the large distance, quickly. He was within a couple hundred miles of Mexico and he might have made it, but for a dog.

In the middle of the street in downtown Congress, Arizona, a barking cattle dog alerted everyone to Jack's presence on the day in April 1896 when he rode into town. Barking and nipping at Davis's horse, it was sufficiently annoying that Davis shot it.

And with that, Diamondfield Jack's days at liberty ended for a long time.

A tearful boy, the dog's owner, quickly found a police officer, who was easily able to locate Jack Davis. Davis might have been able to escape that scrape with a fine and an apology, but he was spooked by the arrival of the officer: He pulled his gun on the officer and disarmed him, and did the same to a second officer who showed up. Plenty of other people were armed as well, however, and one public-spirited citizen pulled his weapon and shot Davis with a well-aimed bullet that didn't kill but did knock him down.

Mainly for his behavior toward the cops, Jack Davis—traveling under the name of Frank Woodson and held by officials who knew nothing of the murder case building to the north—was sentenced to a year in prison. He was manacled and shipped to Yuma, to spend time at one of the most notoriously awful prisons in the old West, the Arizona Territorial.

Davis did not settle down there; he may have realized that law enforcement across the jurisdictional lines might soon figure out what had happened. He escaped on one occasion, briefly, but after three hours at large in Yuma he was back in prison, and in solitary confinement. Returned to the normal prison population, he was soon in a fight with another prisoner, and was sent back to solitary.

He was in confinement when Cassia County Sheriff Oliver Anderson, with two deputized sheepmen in tow, finally showed up. He and others in Idaho had just figured out where Davis was, around the time Davis's original sentence was due to end in March 1897. Anderson was carrying a warrant for his extradition to Idaho on charges of the murders of Cummings and Wilson.

The case was listed as the state against Jack Davis, but it turned into something more expansive—two large teams arrayed against each other, even apart from the teams of lawyers. Davis discovered that the promise the cattlemen had made to their operatives—that they would stand behind them no matter what—was sound. John Sparks, who ran the Sparks-Harrell ranch, hired the attorney widely regarded as the best Idaho had seen since the territory was first created: James Hawley, a Boisean who had handled hundreds of criminal cases—more than three hundred in his whole career, he once estimated. He was famed as one of the best attorneys anywhere in the West. And he wasn't alone: The cattlemen hired others to help him. One of them was Kirtland Perky, a former law associate of William Jennings Bryan, and a future senator from Idaho. If they wanted to demonstrate to other gunmen that they would stand up for their own, they did it impressively.

The sheepmen were no less determined, and they had backing from large portions of the state's political establishment, and—widespread word had it—leaders of the Church of Jesus Christ of Latter-Day Saints, of which the murdered sheepmen were members. They bought legal talent, too, even though the case was technically under the jurisdiction of the Cassia County prosecutor, John Rogers. The sheepmen wanted more insurance, so they made sure that first one special prosecutor from Utah was added to the case, and then another from Boise. The Boisean was a hot young attorney, fast rising in the law and in politics both, named William Borah.

The case opened for trial in Albion before a jury of a dozen men, all farmers but for one miner. All of the jurors lived among the sheepmen and sympathized with them. They represented most of the people in Cassia County; Albion, the county seat, was a central town for the sheepmen.

The trial proceeded predictably, with evidence piling up about Jack Davis's conflicts with the sheepmen, many of whom were called to testify.

Hawley delivered a powerful rebuttal, which made a strong case that Davis was too far south from the murder site in early February of 1896 to have committed the crime. He developed several arguments for Davis's innocence. But the outcome may have been set from the beginning, even without the career-making case developed by the future senator Borah. After discussing the case for three hours, the jury returned to the court with a determination that Davis was guilty of murder.

Judge C. O. Stockslager sentenced Davis to be hanged, two months hence.

Hawley appealed to the Supreme Court. It upheld the sentence. Davis was rescheduled for the noose.

Only then did the cattlemen's real willingness to help Davis emerge. Ranch manager Bower went public, telling the story of how he and Jeff Gray had visited the sheep camp, and how Gray had shot the herders— in self-defense, he said.

Hawley took that confession to the pardons and parole board. The board reaffirmed that Davis had to hang.

That didn't stop the Cassia County prosecutors from trying Bower and Gray for the murders of Cummings and Wilson, or a jury from acquitting them on grounds of self-defense.

Hawley kept appealing for Davis, now in federal courts, where he finally began to win some rulings. He sought a new trial in Cassia County; it was denied. More appeals to the state parole board led to new dates for execution, until the board reversed itself and sentenced Davis to life imprisonment instead. Finally, in December of 1902, after reviewing the case over and over, the pardons and parole board formally pardoned Davis for the crime the state of Idaho still maintained he had committed.

When Diamondfield Jack Davis was released from the rock penitentiary building east of Boise, he hit the road. He walked about a mile toward town, stopping at the city's new natatorium, where he shared a few drinks with his attorney, Hawley, who was now Boise's mayor.

Then he made his way to the train station, and took trains south to Tonopah, Nevada.

He never did find diamond fields. But, scouting the hills around Tonopah, he did find some precious metals and had the one big stroke of luck in his life. For a short time Jack Davis became a wealthy man, a prominent citizen in central Nevada, and he was even renowned for breaking up a lynch mob at one point.

But his wealth and his health soon dissipated, and Davis became, again, another Western wanderer. He died in 1949, after being hit by a taxicab in Las Vegas.

The Montpelier Job

The sun was beating down, the air drifting from nearby Bear Lake was humid, and most people in Montpelier kept to the shade as three horsemen rode into town with a sorrel pack mare tagging behind. It was a hot August afternoon. The horsemen slowly rode down Washington Street, which split Montpelier in two—Mormon on one side, Gentile on the other. They seemed in no hurry and they drew little attention, save for the quality of the men's clothes and the horses' tack, both of which were favorably noted by the few people who saw them enter town.

Inside the Bank of Montpelier, where it was still cool and a little dark—most of the blinds having been pulled to keep out the hot sun—the staff was preparing to shut down for the day. The hour of three in the afternoon having arrived, cashier E. C. Gray lowered the window blinds and prepared to lock up, as soon as the customers inside could be persuaded to leave.

The four customers—one of them a city council member, William Perkins—were cheerily conversing and in no mood to return to the heat outside. Gray and his assistant, Bud McIntosh, needed to start their daily bookkeeping, and that couldn't begin till the doors were locked.

That was when the horsemen rode up to the front of the bank. They dismounted, and one of them walked the horses to the rear of the bank. The leader of the group, a stocky blond man with a broad, thick mustache and a relaxed manner, and his helper, taller, dark-haired, tense, and much more prone to itchy violence, slipped in through the front door.

Once inside, the two robbers immediately pulled out their guns. The leader moved to the side of the front door, his back to the wall, keeping everyone in the room in sight. He seemed calm, still relaxed, but his seriousness was unmistakable.

He spoke in a monotone: "Put your hands up, and keep your mouths shut. Face the closest wall. And keep your hands where I can see them."

Everyone did.

The tall man, who was in the middle of the lobby area, took a few long steps to the counter, where McIntosh had just been and was now frozen in place. He held open a sack and ordered the banker to throw all of the money into it.

McIntosh was young and new at the bank, but he figured he knew something the robbers didn't. He knew that below the counter, placed for just such an emergency, was a Winchester rifle. On hearing the tall man's order for the cash, McIntosh paused, indecisive—*to go for the rifle or not?*—and the tall man sensed the situation. He swung his revolver at McIntosh, smacking him in the forehead and knocking him back.

McIntosh paused again. The robber aimed to take another swing.

His leader, still leaning back against the front wall, called out: "Just get the money."

The tall man pushed McIntosh aside, held open his sack and dumped paper money and gold into it. He also grabbed a second bag, placed on the counter to prove to customers the bank's solvency; he opened it and added to it a handful of gold coins, and then a stack of silver coins as well. They, and the bankers, would calculate later that they had taken more than $7,000 in cash, coin, and metal. But the accounting for the day was not complete; some of it was not reflected in the records, and by some estimates the robbers were said to have gotten $16,500.

There was more in the vault and in other drawers. The tall man was looking around for possibilities when the leader instructed him again.

"That's enough," he said. "We're done here."

Pointing in a fluid motion with his gun, he directed customers and staff into a little group, toward the back of the bank. Then he quietly told them no one would be harmed as long as they kept quiet for ten minutes. Having said that, he and the tall robber slipped out through the back door.

Gray, McIntosh, and the four customers listened intently at the back door. They could make out four horses leaving—they figured it must have been a gang of four, but they were not racing away. They seemed to be taking their time while departing. They had placed the money in pouches carried by the pack mare. After leaving town the mare often chose her own route, sometimes miles from the three robbers on the lam, who tracked her from a distance. They didn't hold the money personally until the point, a couple of days later, when they split up.

Back in the bank, the quiet and scared hostages waited several minutes before trying to rouse an alarm. Feelings of disbelief raged in their heads, along with the questions of who the men were and why they left with little rush. The identity of the robbers was for some time a big mystery, and their greatest success.

Once the sound of hoofbeats had faded, Gray carefully opened the back door and saw none of the robbers. He ran through the bank and dashed out the front door, to the telegraph office. He sent a wire to Paris, a town about ten miles away where the sheriff's office was located.

Jeff Davis, the sheriff of Bear Lake County, arrived at the bank by about four o'clock. By five, he had collected a posse and had learned which way the robbers had left town. The robbers headed east from downtown through Montpelier Canyon, southeast of town, and in the general direction of the Wyoming state line. A posse headed out after them.

The robbery crew was led by a man born Robert Leroy Parker but now better known through much of the West as Butch Cassidy. The crew also included Elza Lay (the tall man) and Bob Meeks (the holder of the horses).

Unlike many gangs of the day, this one had two advantages. One was Cassidy's careful planning based on years of robbing banks. He used his old trick of stationing a group of refresher horses several miles outside of town, to give their escape speed an extra boost and to make identification more difficult.

The other advantage, which had been outside Cassidy's control but was most important, was that the bankers and Idaho law enforcement thought they knew who had robbed the bank. They were sure the gang leader was Tom McCarty, who was both known for robbing banks and known personally in Montpelier, though he did not rob banks locally. McCarty's hangout, and a place where he and his gang found themselves welcome, was Star Valley, a remote pocket of Wyoming northeast of Montpelier. People in Montpelier knew of him partly because he had met and married his wife there.

Gray and Davis figured McCarty's visit to Montpelier had put the small town on the robber's professional horizon, though they did consider it odd that he would strike in a place where he was so well known. They might also have paused to consider that no one in Montpelier had said they recognized him as one of the robbers.

Davis and his posse rode hard up to Star Valley—about 90 degrees away from the direction the Cassidy gang had taken—and looked around the region searching for McCarty and his men. The closest they came was a sorrel mare that seemed to resemble one of the animals spotted in Montpelier, but the lawmen were unable catch her to examine more carefully.

The posse, dispirited, gave up and returned to Montpelier. Soon after, Davis raised another posse and tried again, probing around the Wyoming border for news of McCarty.

Then, from visitors to town, came word about three ranch hands who had been working in Wyoming well south of Star Valley and had gone missing just before the Montpelier robbery. Davis reviewed the descriptions of the Montpelier robbers, the McCarty gang, and the ranch hands. And he began to realize that none of them matched nearly closely enough. Only later did the reality begin to sink in. And only several weeks later was he able to make an arrest.

The Montpelier foray into Idaho notwithstanding, Butch Cassidy was not, for the most part, a bank robber.

Robert Leroy Parker, still his legal identity, was said to have chosen his nom de crime partly in memory of an old friend and partly for occupational description—he was a butcher of stolen cattle, an occupation he set up visibly in Rock Springs, Wyoming. (He was said to have adopted a pseudonym in the interest of not embarrassing members of his family, who still lived in Utah.) But from his early twenties he had been involved in the occasional bank knockoff, and he turned more in that direction after his arrest for rustling in Wyoming in 1894. In January of 1896, released from prison, he decided that cattle theft didn't pay so well.

So he started scouting banks. And on August 13, seven months after his release from prison, he engineered one of the most successful robberies of his career, in a small, remote, quiet town in southeast Idaho. The bank recovered well enough. The Bank of Montpelier had a more successful run than many of its type in its era—banks in those days came and went quickly—but it finally failed in 1925, owing to "unfounded rumors" about its solvency.

The robbery had a specific motivation, almost altruistic, because most of the money wasn't headed for the robbers' own pockets. Among the friends of the robbers was a colleague named Matt Warner, then jailed in Utah on a charge of murder. Records of the time and since suggest Warner had been framed, and Cassidy and his crew certainly believed as much. The bulk of the paper and gold from Montpelier, which may have amounted to $16,000 or perhaps more, was spent on Warner's legal defense. It had some effect as Warner wound up with a relatively short prison term.

Cassidy apparently never returned to Idaho. He usually did not return to old haunts for additional robberies.

Meeks did come back to Idaho, but then he had no say in the matter—he was the only one of the three robbers actually arrested, convicted, and jailed for the Montpelier robbery. His misfortune started with mistaken identity. In Cheyenne a few weeks after the Montpelier holdup, a railroad detective spotted him and thought he might have been one of the robbers on a recent rail heist. Meeks wasn't, and he offered an alibi for the rail job. In doing so, however, he had to acknowledge that he was close to Montpelier on August 13, 1896, the day of the Montpelier bank job, and that attracted attention from Idaho law enforcement. The case against him was soon put together, and through it the true background of the robbery, including Butch Cassidy's involvement, became public.

Alfred Budge, the Bear Lake County prosecutor, crafted an effective case against Meeks. He was tried in Idaho, where Gray testified against him though he admitted he hadn't seen him inside the bank. The jury convicted Meeks. The case was a key early win for Budge, who went on to a great Idaho legal career, eventually serving for many years on the Idaho Supreme Court. In late 1897 Meeks was sent to the Idaho State Penitentiary in Boise.

Meeks became a well-known prisoner there. He attempted escape twice, losing a leg on the second occasion when he was shot during the attempt. Released in 1912, he seems to have wandered east to Colorado, where he took a job as a ranch manager.

A few years after the Montpelier heist, Lay was imprisoned for another robbery in New Mexico. That seems to have been his last illicit escapade, however. In midlife he changed direction and became a moderately successful businessman, mainly through his investments in oil operations and properties. He lived a quiet life until his death in 1933.

As for Butch Cassidy, some say he went to South America with a gunman he later hooked up with, Harry Lombaugh—the "Sundance Kid"—and died in Bolivia. Or maybe he dropped out of sight and lived out his life anonymously in some remote place in western America. As is the case with so many facts about Butch Cassidy, no one really knows for sure.

In Levy's Alley

Levy's Alley was a part of town where the respectable people of Boise didn't go, and if they did, they sure didn't want to be seen there. Joe Leonard was among those who, for financial reasons, had little choice. He'd lived in the rundown building at 612 Main Street off and on as he patched together an income. The building's insides were dark, grimy, and dank.

But on an early October day in 1901, his fortunes had improved enough to find better lodging, and he was at the building this Saturday to see if a friend, Matt Bilbrey, was looking to move out as well. He was thinking about lunch, too, since the time was just before noon.

Opening the front door and stepping inside from the cool early October weather, looking up at the stairway to the second floor, Leonard took a whiff and smelled it immediately—something damp, corrupted, and putrid. He hesitated and considered turning around, but then started up the stairs anyway. He'd ask Matt about it.

Not that bad smells were entirely unusual in this place. Two blocks in the city of Boise, on the east end of downtown and close by Fort Boise military outpost, constituted the red light district, and this build-ing was its centerpiece. Often nicknamed for the walkway to its rear—Levy's Alley—it served a dual purpose. Some of the Main Street rooms were rented on the cheap, often to hardscrabble working men like Leonard and Bilbrey, usually men new to town who got out as soon as they could. The other rooms, especially the back rooms that faced the alley, were Boise's largest bordello.

Davis Levy, bone thin and hunched over, possessor of a sickly mien and body odor widely remarked, was one of three building owners in the area; the others were a man named Broadbent and a woman named Ellen Bush, who collected substantial "rent" from the prostitutes who lived and worked in the close-packed cribs barely out of view of Main Street. As Leonard stepped up the creaking stairs and reached the landing, he glanced at the window to the right, the sliding glass pane behind which Levy would often sit, opening it to take his payments from the tenants, then slamming it shut again, usually with a curse.

A small curtain was pulled over it, and Leonard saw no light inside.

He bore right down the hallway snaking around Levy's room, and then left, the smell getting worse as he went.

Leonard knocked on Bilbrey's door and roused the occupant, who'd had his own window open and hadn't noticed the smell—until now.

Leonard asked Bilbrey the origin of the smell, but Bilbrey said he had no idea. They speculated it might be a body, dead and decaying. Leonard thought about knocking on Levy's door and asking him, but Bilbrey remarked that Levy hadn't been seen since sometime Thursday afternoon. And then the thought hit both of them.

Leonard jogged back down the stairs and out into the street, gulping fresh air as he went. He looked around for someone he knew and thought he could trust, and fastened on Charles Logan, a Boisean he'd met some time ago. He explained the situation at Levy's Alley, and Logan agreed to come with him. They collected Bilbrey and tried the doors to Levy's apartment as well as the payment window, but they were locked. Logan suggested knocking down the door, but the other two rejected that idea. Logan suggested that, in that case, the other two should keep a watch, and he would try to find a police officer.

Within a few minutes he had returned with the chief of police, Ben Francis, and an officer named Byron. Both of them knew of the building and knew about Levy. Only the previous spring they had been to the building to serve criminal charges against him for permitting a house of prostitution.

They shouted through the door but got no response. Byron had a master key that worked on many of the locks in downtown Boise, but it did no good on this one.

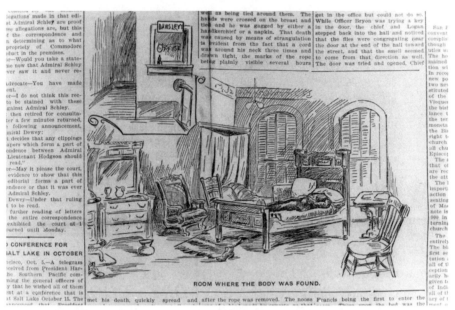

ROOM WHERE THE BODY WAS FOUND.

A sketch of the room that Davis Levy's body was found in
Courtesy Idaho State Historical Society

Then Francis, looking around the hallway, saw that flies seemed to be headed to another door, to the room next to Levy's apartment, room 13. The smell seemed strongest from that room. Byron tried his master key on the door to this room, and it worked. Francis and then Byron stepped in, and when they saw what was inside, they held Leonard and Bilbrey back.

The room was not Levy's personally. He had sometimes said that— although he owned the building—he couldn't afford what it usually cost. It was bigger than other rooms in the building, was well-appointed with new furniture, a stove, and a closet, and it had two large windows overlooking Main Street and a large bed angled between them. It was a room for a tenant of some means.

It had no renter at the moment, though. Its immediate occupant was Davis Levy, and he was on the bed, dead, and in a condition of serious decay. Next to his body were six keys, carefully arranged from the head to the foot; a small money bag, empty, was found at the foot of the bed. A bloody towel covered Levy's face. His hands and feet were bound with an unusual type of rope, which police soon learned was ordinarily seen in the area only as a securer of boxes containing bananas.

Levy's death became the most spectacular murder case in Boise history.

Police began to decipher the facts of the case. They worked out—from the condition of the body, Levy's last writings, and the testimony of tenants of the building—that he was last seen Thursday afternoon and probably had died that evening. He had been killed by strangulation, with a rope tied around his neck; that helped police later determine that he had been eating his supper when the murder occurred. The killer struck him from behind, the attack so sudden that he'd not even had time to swallow.

They also figured out that Levy had not been in this room, that he had kept it empty and clean for prospective tenants. He had been killed in his own apartment, then dragged—his shoes scuffing the floor and almost falling apart—from there to room 13. The furniture was precisely in place, and had not been touched.

Police searched the office but did not find the $500 in tenant payments they expected to find. Levy collected payments from his tenants, most of them prostitutes, around the first of the month, and ordinarily deposited them by around the fifth or the sixth. The murder had occurred on the third, so most of the money would have been collected but not yet deposited; evidently, the killer knew that. Whatever the motive of the killing, robbery certainly was one of the results.

All this came easily enough. But figuring out the identity of the killer was more tenuous. Rewards—including one from the governor—were offered for information about the case. Levy, after all, had a long history in Boise; he was notorious in the town, and more than a few people were happy to see him gone.

His exact age was uncertain, but Boiseans did know that he was of Jewish background and had emigrated from Poland, along with several relatives, around 1847. No one knew his original name. Most of the Levy family seemed to have migrated to the west, and Davis Levy arrived in Boise about 1868, when the city was still far less than a decade old and inexpensive lots in the growing military and mining supply center were still easy to come by. Levy bought, built, and ran a string of small businesses, starting with the California Bakery. But as years went by over the next third of a century, he found that the location of his buildings at Main and Sixth Streets, close to the military base, had a unique value—that is, if the right "tenants" were maintained there. Levy kept prices low and the cribs small and compact, and the "soiled doves" of the region made their way to him. His building, typically called "Levy's Alley," became, the *Idaho Statesman* said, "Levy's reeking house of vice." For a while the area was called Whitechapel, after the London district where Jack the Ripper did his dirty work.

The city's more patrician elements couldn't decide if they disliked Levy more for the way he made his money or for the way he shook his fist at them, cussing and blaspheming whenever he got the chance—not that he often ventured outside his haunts, which he did less and less as the years went on. The new mayor of Boise, Moses Alexander, may have despised him for another reason—Levy's Jewish background, which Alexander shared but which Alexander was making thoroughly respectable in this small frontier city. Alexander had become a pillar of the community, a highly regarded figure in town who would become not only mayor but governor, at a time when anti-Semitism was not uncommon in small western towns. Alexander and the few other Jewish leaders in town were angry at how Levy and his antics might damage the reputation of the local Jewish community.

But Levy's doors were not locked so tight he could not be shaken from them, as he had been in the spring of 1901, when he was charged by the city of Boise with allowing a house of ill repute to operate in his buildings. He was found guilty and fined $44. Naturally, he appealed. In late summer he went before a jury, rather than a judge, and this time his attorney made the right kinds of arguments. At his appeal, Levy was found not guilty.

Despite Levy's unlawful past, in death he had the law working for him. Officers started with Levy's office, of course, collecting records where they could be found. The search expanded to all the sitting rooms and then to the cribs, upending the usual run of business there. Matt Bilbrey left the building, too, carrying his bicycle, clothes, and personal belongings as fast as he could.

The case made daily headlines, even on those days when, as the *Statesman* admitted, "Nothing of importance developed yesterday in the Levy murder case." Rewards were posted, the Boise police scoured the east end of town for clues, and Boiseans were following matters closely. The pressure was on to make an arrest and bring the case to a close.

Police soon had a man in custody—actually just a boy—eighteen-year-old Grover West. A few days before the murder, he and several others about the same age were talking at a Boise home about the difficulty of finding a job and making money, when West spoke up and said he knew where he could get $10,000 easily. He said Davis Levy had that much lying around his building, and that once earlier he and a partner had tried to break in and get it but were spotted by Levy and chased off. He would try again, he said. Word of this conversation gravitated to the police, who interrogated West for hours but concluded he knew nothing about Levy's death.

By then the police were taking interest in another man whose movements seemed to arouse suspicion, and whose source of income seemed to mesh with Davis Levy's.

George Levy, an immigrant from France and no relation to David, had been seen in downtown Boise the night of October 3. Witnesses placed him at the Weil & Co. tobacco shop from about 8:00 p.m. to 10:30 p.m., after which he hopped a train headed west, and disembarked at Baker City, Oregon. The *Idaho Statesman* jumped to the conclusion that he "could not have done the terrible deed." The paper also concluded, "That there was more than one murde[rer] is patent."

Serious troublemaker George Levy

Courtesy Idaho State Historical Society

The *Statesman* would be proved wrong on both counts.

Unlike Davis, George Levy was at least using his original name; it was given him at his birth in Paris, France, in 1861. He was about forty at the time of the murder. His background in France is unclear, but he was thirty-seven when he came to the United States, older than most immigrants. He spent several months in New York, then traveled to Pittsburgh, then Butte, Montana, and next Spokane. From there he headed to smaller towns, first Walla Walla—where local law enforcement officials strongly urged him to leave the area—and then Baker, and finally, early that summer, Boise.

Wherever he went, he was accompanied by women, two arriving with him in Boise, and between them, they made money. By late October of 1901 he had $2,800 in a bank account at Baker and $200 spending money in his pockets. At Boise, the three found initial living quarters at a house on Bannock Street.

The women did not stay with George Levy long. While still under his supervision, they went to work in the cribs owned by Davis Levy, and the two Levys were thrown into a business relationship. It did not go well, or last long. The two were seen in fierce arguments, and soon George Levy and his prostitutes were out of the cribs and law enforcement had descended on them. George Levy, knowing about the building owner's legal troubles, offered evidence against him, but the police issued an order demanding he get out of town. That may have been a result of communications with police in other cities. But George Levy was certain that Davis Levy was behind the order, and he was cursing him and swearing vengeance even as he and his two prostitutes hopped the train west back to Baker.

George Levy was prone to violence and inexplicable behavior. One story making the rounds, even before his arrest for murder, was that he recently had captured a live wild rabbit, which he injured and then skinned alive to watch it suffer.

George Levy's later testimony didn't make clear how he planned to excuse his appearance at Boise on October 3. But he tried to cover himself with an alibi. In his statement to the police, he said that he met with friends most of that Thursday, then had supper at a Boise restaurant at about 6:30 p.m. Within the next hour, he said, he visited Weil's cigar store, circled to his hotel for his valise, returned to Weil's, and stayed there until late evening, when the train was to depart for Baker.

Other witnesses, however, blew holes in that schedule. They said George Levy had left the restaurant earlier than he had indicated, and that he didn't appear at Weil's at all until 8:00 p.m., leaving a span of more than a hour unaccounted for, and during which Davis Levy was probably killed. They also said that when George Levy arrived at Weil's, he tried to act as though he had been there just shortly before, which struck oddly the people there who knew he hadn't been.

Police Chief Ben Francis and two others took the train to Baker themselves on October 21, tracked down Levy, and arrested him and the two women, cousins Alice and Jennie Mitchell, he was then traveling with. They may have gotten there just in time. George Levy had just bought a train ticket and he was headed east to Rock Springs, Wyoming, which meant passing through Idaho but also probably headed in the direction law enforcement might least expect. Levy tried to say that he was simply headed back to Boise, but one of the women, interviewed separately, contradicted him.

George Levy was held in the Boise jail. The following February, he was tried for the murder of Davis Levy, and he was convicted. He was sentenced to a term in the Idaho Penitentiary, east of Boise, where he served nine years before his release. The relatively short stretch for a murder conviction may have had something to do with the unsavory nature of the victim. George seems to have vanished from the public record after that.

George Levy's crime did have a significant effect on Boise. When Davis Levy died, his property was first taken over by an administrator named Charles Kahn. His first actions were to research and inventory the property, which threw an unexpected light on the illicit business that had been conducted there. Then Levy's relatives arrived, from San Francisco and Salt Lake City, and when they learned what use the property had been put to, they insisted on cleaning house.

That only matched the pressure from Mayor Alexander, who pushed through the city council a fierce anti-red-light ordinance and ordered police to back it up. A study of the period describes the action: "By a vote of four to three, the council voted in favor of the Mayor's action which included: No 'cribs,' all occupants to be driven out of the city and kept out; no boys to lounge about any place 'where evil may make its habituation'; no red lights, no music, no dancing—nothing to attract attention; women to keep themselves secluded 'just as much as possible.'"

It was as much as was realistic for the times.

The geographic location called Levy's Alley is still noted in Boise, though its history usually is not. These days it is part of what is called Old Boise, a place of boutique shops and trendy restaurants across Main Street from the new city hall building.

Davis Levy wouldn't recognize it.

The Assassin

The man from out of town, just arrived December 13 at the Caldwell station on the eastbound train, seemed nondescript but garrulous, befitting his self-description as a businessman on the make. Walking a half-dozen blocks to the Saratoga Hotel, on the west end of downtown Caldwell, he registered under the name Thomas Hogan. He gave no indication that his real name was Albert Horsley—few people in the western United States knew him that way. But he wanted to be sure he was not associated with a name quite a few people in Idaho, and several other states, did know: Harry Orchard.

He was under casual watch by the locals, as drifters into town generally were. A sizable number of men in those days wandered around the West, drawn to places like Idaho partly because of their precious metals reputations, but would end up finding no jobs, running out of money, and usually drifting on. Most probably assumed Hogan was one of them.

Many of these drifters, even in winter, pitched rough tents where they could find level ground. Others took cheap beds in flophouses. Relatively few were able to manage even the low nightly rent of a hotel room. And so Orchard, who seemed to have no back story and whose reasons for coming to Caldwell were unclear, drew a certain amount of attention. He was well-groomed, clean-shaven, dressed in a three-piece suit, and—unlike most drifters—seemed not to lack for money. He made vague references to being in the sheep business or in real estate, but the overall sense was of mystery. He spent a good deal of time at the Saratoga, playing cards.

Around Christmas, some of the guests noticed that he seemed to have grown increasingly nervous. They would have been shocked had they known why: He was plotting the assassination of one of Caldwell's best-liked citizens, former governor Frank Steunenberg, at his house in town. And his first attempt had failed.

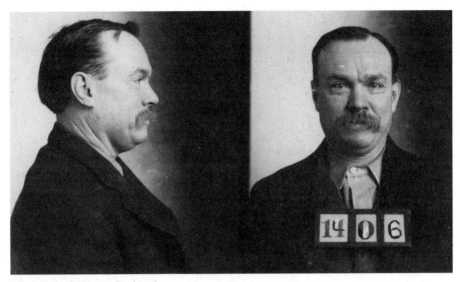

Mugshot of Harry Orchard
Courtesy Idaho State Historical Society

"We did not go very close to there in the day-time," Orchard would say a few months later. "We went past the front of his house at night. We located him one afternoon in the Saratoga Hotel. He stayed there until dark. We went up after dark and placed the bomb alongside of the sidewalk leading to his house with a wire across the sidewalk so that when he walked along this he would hit this and explode the bomb. . . . The wire being attached to a stick across the sidewalk about four inches or so above the sidewalk, and that when he walked into this wire it would turn the windlass and the bottle, but this time our plans miscarried.

"Before attaching this wire across there and after it was all fixed I went back to the hotel to see if he was still there and found he was. When he started to come home I went ahead of him and fastened the wire across the sidewalk. Simpkins [Orchard's fellow conspirator] was back at the hotel. And then I went back to the hotel as fast as I could after attaching this wire. After half an hour we went back to see what had happened to this and found the wire had been broken and found that the bottle was upright and had not spilled any acid on the caps. I took the bomb up again and took it away with me, and took it across the railroad and buried it in some manure in the stock-yards. We had it in a box."

His prompt to try again came on Saturday, January 30, about dusk, with Steunenberg's regular visit to the Saratoga. Steunenberg was there to pick up a *Caldwell Tribune,* the newspaper edited and published by the Steunenberg family. Every Saturday, the former governor would pick up a copy near the hotel's front door and read it at the bar in the back. After learning Steunenberg was in the building, soon to head home, Orchard decided his chance had come. He quit the card game, raced to his room, collected the bomb, and carried it—carefully and surreptitiously, he hoped—to Steunenberg's front gate. He set it and returned to the Saratoga, and got back into the card game.

When he overheard that Steunenberg was leaving, he couldn't resist. He had to leave and watch. With the governor walking briskly a couple of blocks ahead, Orchard hung back, keeping him barely in sight. He paused as Steunenberg approached his front yard and reached for the gate.

And then, as he stood frozen in place, Orchard saw the bomb explode.

Harry Orchard turned and ran as fast as he could back to the Saratoga. He rejoined the card game, trying to keep the wind out of his breath. He looked unemotional as word of the assassination rippled through the crowd. And then he went to the dining room to eat his supper.

The very first time Harry Orchard told the story, signed with his surprisingly ornate signature, of how he came to blow up former Idaho governor Frank Steunenberg by dynamite at his house in Caldwell, was on January 27, 1906, to private Pinkerton detectives James McParland and George Huebner. The Pinkerton National Detective Agency, the largest of its kind in America and by then more than half a century old, was much more than the private investigator firms as we've come to know them in recent decades in fact and fiction. Pinkerton employed hundreds of operatives, some of them as detectives in the usual sense, but many others as henchmen and provocateurs in the employ of governments and corporations. Later, and different, versions of confession appeared in print in years to come.

He called himself Harry Orchard—that was his reply when asked his name—but readily acknowledged he had grown up as Albert Horsley, born around 1867 or 1868 (he was not sure of the date) in a small community in Ontario, Canada.

The weather was typically cold when in November 1895 (or possibly 1896—he was not sure about that either) he quit his job at a cheese factory in Ontario, where other members of his family also worked, to head out on the road, to the mining country. He was far from alone in thinking about making more money in the silver and gold mines of the West, but he was not driven as fiercely as many others. He crossed the border in Detroit, and stayed there a few weeks, but found nothing more than odd jobs.

From there he traveled—probably hopping a freight train in the style of hobos—much further west, back across the border to Nelson, British Columbia. He had heard of good opportunities there, too, but found none. Following the rumor trail, he headed south to Spokane, where he looked for work for about a month and struck out yet again.

One day he saw a sign that led him to follow the job trail again, this time with better luck.

He made his way to Wallace, about eighty miles east of Spokane up in the Coeur d'Alenes. If Orchard was looking for a booming Western community, and one loaded with opportunity, he had finally arrived at the right place. Barely a decade before, massive silver deposits were discovered in the Coeur d'Alene River Basin. The popular story was that prospector Noah Kellogg's mule exposed a rich vein; the story may have been spurious, but the precious metals were real. In popular speech the geographic description "the Coeur d'Alenes" was about to be replaced by "Silver Valley," its shorthand description even today. A batch of towns sprang up from nowhere—Wallace, Kellogg, Gem, Osburn, Burke, Wardner, Mullen, and many others—and became a combustible mixture of mine owners and claimants, and hundreds, then thousands, of mine workers. Idaho had seen plenty of mining boomtowns before, but this one promised more permanence: These silver finds were clearly massive enough to last decades. And they did.

Orchard worked for the Markwell Brothers for most of the next year, driving a milk wagon between the mining towns of Wallace and Burke, until about Christmas. Then he saw another opportunity. Taking about $150—or thereabouts—of his savings from his wages, he bought a small coal yard at Burke, and a team of horses. Many homeowners had coal delivered to their homes for fireplaces and stoves, and Orchard started making those deliveries in the Burke area. He prospered, and after a couple of years even put down money on a sixteenth interest in a mine, the Hercules Mine near Wallace.

Orchard never said, and there's no remaining record of, what happened to his business. But after a couple of years, he sold it and took a mining job at the Tiger & Poorman Mine in the Burke area. More critically, in early 1899, shortly after starting work there, he joined the Burke Lodge of the Western Federation of Miners.

The Western Federation of Miners was a very active, and sometimes radical, organization in the 1890s, and took seriously the idea that miners across the West were bound to act in support of each other. The Tiger & Poorman was a peaceful enough workplace where the union and management got along. But a few miles to the south, relations at a mine at Wardner became increasingly tense over wages and working conditions.

"We were stopped from going to work and were called to attend a meeting of the Union early in the morning of the 29th of April," Orchard recalled. At the meeting union leaders said the whole lodge was expected to go to Wardner in support of the miners. Headed there,

Orchard noted a lot of firearms in the hands of law enforcement, private detectives, and miners.

On the way, one of the federation leaders asked for help in carrying explosive powder deep into the Wardner mine. Orchard volunteered and helped haul it, and said later that he was around when the mine was blown up. National leaders at the Western Federation, he was told, wanted it done. That explosion triggered some of the most violent episodes of the labor conflict at the mines.

To this point, Harry Orchard had no record of violence at all, but when it came he willingly participated, and more than that, volunteered. He did not seem to think any of it especially remarkable; he seemed to absorb it like a passing pageant.

Along with some of the union leaders, Orchard got out of the way after the Warner mine blew up. Troops were called into the Silver Valley, and many of the miners were held in a large, open bullpen. Along with others, Orchard observed the activity from the hills overlooking Wallace.

Having watched the Coeur d'Alenes deteriorate into violence, Orchard decided to move on. But rather than find a conventional salary job, he saw in the union violence a new professional opportunity. He headed east through Montana, catching rides and working a few odd jobs, until he reached Butte, the region center of organized miner laborers.

But it wasn't until he took work in Colorado that Orchard turned to violence that would lead to fatalities. He was prepared to take his violent protests to the next level. At one mine, Orchard said that his specific job was to make a bomb to be thrown into one of the coal bunkers at the Vindicator Mine. He built and threw the device, but it failed to ignite. Still, the willingness to kill seemed to have been ignited.

Orchard recalled years later, "Adams and I stayed in Denver for a couple of days and during that time the executive board of the Western Federation of Miners was in session, in 1904. [A man named] Gregory came into Denver that morning. I have been told he was some kind of a deputy sheriff under Billy Reno, a detective, and had been guarding the

Colorado Fuel and Iron company's mines during the strike. It was reported there in Denver that he was the chief of those followers that was beating up the officers of the United Miner Workers of America. This came up in the executive board. . . .

"I went back to my room on 38th Street and got my sawed-off shotgun. . . . We followed him up the street and when we got opposite the alley he stopped ahead of us a little piece, turned around and backed up as though reaching for a gun. Thereupon we shot him three times; I did the shooting. . . . [Bill] Haywood said it was a damn good smooth job."

After that, Orchard said, he was assigned to blow up a railroad depot, and did, reportedly killing fourteen people. He was sent out on the road again, in the fall of 1904, this time to San Francisco to murder Fred Bradley, an executive of the Bunker Hill & Sullivan Mine. Bradley was away, traveling in Alaska, but Orchard stayed in the city for "four or five months," receiving pay from Denver. Finally he put together a lead pipe bomb, five inches long with a string attached so that when the string was disturbed, it would explode. Just as Bradley returned home, Orchard said, he placed the bomb, and it went off. But it turned out not to be quite powerful enough; Bradley was wounded but recovered.

Orchard's next job would make him an international figure.

There's no certainty about how the plot came about. In his confessions to detectives in 1906, Orchard said this: "[Charles] Moyer, Haywood, George Pettibone and I had a conference some time in August 1905, in Denver, Colorado, in Moyer's office, and it was decided by us that I come down to Idaho and try to assassinate ex-Governor Steunenberg. I told them I would have to have some money to start with. Haywood gave me $300. I started in a couple of days and came to Nampa. I bought a return ticket from Denver to Portland and returned via Seattle, and came to Nampa and stayed there two or three days and stopped at the Commercial Hotel. There was no one with me at that time. I went to Caldwell from there and stopped at the Pacific Hotel and learned where ex-Governor Steunenberg lived."

The extent of Moyer's, Haywood's, and Pettibone's involvement in the assassination has been hotly debated ever since. Some suggest they simply spoke harshly about Steunenberg, and Orchard took it from there. Others argue that Orchard was not strong enough a personality to undertake such an important killing on his own.

Orchard easily learned Steunenberg's business and daily patterns. He mostly was through with politics (though he apparently was thinking about a comeback), but he periodically visited the state capital of Boise for business reasons and usually stayed at the Idanha Hotel there. Orchard went there, and soon "I had a skeleton key, or a pass key, whatever you might call it. I intended to take the bomb and put it under his bed in a grip fixed with a clock so that when the alarm went off it would cause it to explode. When I got to thinking about it on my way to Nampa I thought it was so big that it would possibly kill half the people in the hotel. I abandoned the idea, intending to come back again at some later period. I left Nampa then and went to Portland and took my trunk with me."

That fall Orchard quietly returned to the Silver Valley and met with another union activist there, Jack Simpkins. In November, having discussed the bombing idea, they decided to return to southwest Idaho.

Simpkins may not have made the trip, but Orchard did. And, after some additional preparation, he built a bomb. After one failed attempt, he reset it in place at Steunenberg's house, and it blew up Steunenberg.

The rest of the story became internationally known.

Orchard, registered as Tom Hogan, kept his room at the Saratoga Hotel and kept on playing cards, though after New Year's some people did notice he was beginning to drink a little more heavily. He was briefly questioned by police and then, hearing he was a suspect, walked into the city's police station and insisted on clearing himself. The police were more suspicious than ever, and the next day, in the middle of a card game, he was arrested and jailed.

Soon after Orchard was caught and publicly unmasked as the killer, he confessed. He implicated three Denver union leaders, Bill Haywood,

Charles Moyer, and Bill Pettibone, whose resulting trial months later became an international sensation; Orchard's testimony was pivotal to the case against them. Further drama was added because the attorneys involved were the renowned Clarence Darrow and future senator William Borah, who were on opposite sides in the case. The three labor leaders were acquitted, but Orchard's conviction stuck.

Orchard entered the Idaho State Penitentiary in 1908 and stayed there for forty-six years, the longest sentence ever served in the original penitentiary.

The assassin was originally sentenced to hang, just a couple of years after the trial. But as the months went on, Orchard told any and all who would listen how he had been born again and saw the evil in his past for what it was. The state parole board cut his sentence to life in prison. Later, it was cut still further: He was offered parole. He did not accept, preferring to tend his gardens and live out his days in the place he had come to think of as home.

In 1954, Orchard died at the Idaho State Penitentiary.

Deadshot

On that bright morning in late July, Albert and Homer Carr rode their horses slowly and quietly to the slaughterhouse outside Pierce—the butchering operation partly run by Bill Reed. They were not eager to be there, but their visit had a purpose. The night before, Ben Craig, who lived at Pierce, had ridden to the Carr ranch to tell Dan Carr, the boys' father, that some of the family's cattle had been stolen. Not only that, one had been butchered, and its carcass, with the ranch's brand intact, was hanging in the slaughterhouse.

Bill Reed was a man no one in town wanted to cross, and to this point no one had. His background was hazy, but he seemed a hard type. He was said to have been a lawman, and was also said to have killed people without benefit of a badge. And his skill with a gun, whether rifle or handgun, was locally known to be unmatched.

The brothers decided that Homer Carr would stand guard at the slaughterhouse while Albert rode into Pierce to locate Reed.

Reed was not hard to find. He was at the City Hotel, his usual haunt, and he was not alone. Ever since coming to town two years before, Reed usually was seen in the company of some combination of three other men. One was his business partner, whom he called "Kid" Moore. The others were A. J. Sloan and Chester Rice, two cattlemen who worked the area and whose cattle often grazed around the prairie in the Pierce and Weippe area. On this day, Albert Carr spotted Reed and Rice walking out of the City Hotel. He dismounted and walked up to them.

Carr told him the story, that cattle had been stolen and that he had seen a branded hide at Reed's slaughterhouse. A signal seemed to pass between Reed and Rice. Silently, Rice mounted his horse and rode off to the slaughterhouse. There he found Homer Carr, on guard; rather than confront him, he decided to turn back.

93

The town of Pierce, Idaho
Courtesy Idaho State Historical Society

Reed and the younger Carr were still talking. The older man didn't seem threatening as he was trying to calm Carr, suggesting that he was trying to find out what happened and that he didn't want to get into a big dispute. Reed was trying to establish himself as a meat vendor and a respectable businessman; he also did some work at the Salings Butcher Shop in Pierce. He wanted to put down roots here. He suggested that they all head back to the slaughterhouse and look at the goods.

There was no mistake about the hide. It was clearly marked with the Carr ranch's distinctive "76" brand.

Reed insisted he had nothing to do with stealing any cattle and that he simply slaughtered and butchered what was brought in for him. The Carrs shot back that even if it wasn't Reed, it was probably those other three he ran with—Moore, Rice, and Sloan. Rice and Sloan owned and grazed cattle in the area, and Moore fed cattle for owners around the region. They could easily swipe a few from another operator.

Reed dismissed the idea. When a livery man named Emmet Barrows showed up, Reed told him to haul the meat from the disputed animal back to the butcher shop he ran at Pierce—it would spoil otherwise; the Carrs, he said, could have the hide. The Carrs insisted it all stay where it was, so their father could come by and inspect it.

Reed then demanded the Carrs produce a legal warrant, if they had one. They didn't. Reed then pulled his gun on them, repeating that the hide was theirs but the meat was headed to the butcher's shop in Pierce.

Dan Carr sought out law enforcement, thin at Pierce and even at the nearest town, Orofino, because the sheriff and prosecutors were based almost eighty miles away at Lewiston. He swore out complaints against the four—Reed, Moore, Rice, and Sloan—on a charge of grand larceny of a two-year-old cow, and insisted they be arrested. A court hearing was held two days later, on the last day of July, at which Sloan and Rice appeared and pleaded not guilty, but Reed and Moore did not. A few days later, Reed surrendered himself to a constable named Miles Cochran at Orofino, where he was allowed to stay free on condition he show at the next court hearing.

The prosecutor, Daniel Needham, then filed the case in Lewiston, demanding the trial be held there. This was a red flag; Reed's honed gunman instincts told him this was a setup and a trap, and he decided to bolt. Reed held the local constable at bay with his gun and tied him up to win a head start.

He met up with Moore, Rice, and Sloan, outside of town and on the run. Reed recalled saying: "Boys, we're all outlaws now. There are warrants out for all of us. So we better hightail it out of here."

Soon they saw Constable Cochran firing at them. Like swatting a mosquito, they stopped and fired back, and soon Cochran, who had no other assistance, turned back to Orofino. Again, they seemed in the clear and continued.

Before long a larger posse materialized. The Carr brothers, Albert and Homer, and their father, Dan, were deputized with instructions to bring the four to justice "dead or alive," and they soon rounded up more help. Hearing that Reed and the others were on the road not far from the Carr ranch, they took a shortcut through the woods and pulled up out of sight. Dan Carr explored down the road, finally deciding on an ambush near a watering trough called Carr Springs, commonly used by travelers. There they waited.

He did not have to wait long. Soon, Reed and his three friends rode their horses into the clearing and to the trough, to water them for the next stage of the trip. Reed was behind the others, keeping a close watch on the scene, but he failed to observe the ambushers. The Carrs waited until Reed had pulled his horse up to the water, and then let loose with fire.

One of the first shots hit Reed in his right arm, knocking his rifle off into the grass. The horses reared and whinnied, and all but Reed's, which still was mounted, started to run at random. Carr fired again, bullets catching Sloan and Kid Moore.

Dan emerged from the forest, thinking the shooting was done, or if not, that he could finish it now.

Reed had just gotten his horse under control, whipped off his bandanna and tied it around his arm, and dismounted behind the horse. Carr tried to aim at him. But Reed began to demonstrate just why he was so respected as a gunman. His own severe wound barely slowing him, he now reached around for a second rifle, pulled it up, and fired. He inflicted a shallow flesh wound on Carr, who now started to back up and head for shelter. Reed gave him none. Reed fired again, sending him sprawling to the ground, and then shot him yet again to finish the work. Four shots, no misses, with his right arm incapacitated.

And then he surveyed the damage. Kid Moore, his partner—likely his brother—had been shot to death. Sloan was injured in his neck, but the wound was manageable. It was more manageable than Reed's own; his arm was going to require a physician's help soon.

The three remaining horsemen, Sloan, Reed, and Rice, took off on a side road, but after little more than a mile, Reed could travel no further. He became delirious and then lost consciousness. The other two, thinking he was dying, left him there and took off for a cabin Rice owned in the forests above Orofino.

They probably thought that was a little-known location, but it was known well enough for another sheriff's posse, this one headed up directly by law enforcement officials, to find it and stake it out. When they caught Sloan and Rice there, peacefully, the two described where they had left Reed.

Reed later told that he continued to walk through the mountains to a remote cabin where the residents tried to help mend him, but where he was soon found by the police. About a week after starting their flight, Reed was checked into the five-year-old St. Joseph's Hospital at Lewiston.

Bill Reed was born in San Antonio, Texas. His parents died young, and he was raised on a remote Texas ranch. He said that he shot to death a man—who happened to be his school teacher—when he was only thirteen, and then fled to South America. On his return, he said, charges were dropped and he became first a Texas Ranger because of his great skill with a firearm, and then an entertainer in cowboy shows. No one has disputed his stint as a Texas Ranger, because somewhere in his early life, he picked up an extraordinary skill with guns.

Still, there was no whiff of celebrity about him when he and Kid Moore, who is believed to have been his brother (though Reed seems not to have specifically confirmed this), rode into northern Idaho in 1905, two more drifters on the lookout for work.

Moore was content working at odd jobs, mainly helping out some of the area ranchers delivering feed for the cattle grazing on and around the Weippe Prairie. Reed, however, seems to have had in mind a more stable existence. He wanted to put down roots, run some cattle of his own, maybe even set up a business in town. He built a small cabin for himself at Summit, a few miles uphill from Pierce, and began scouting opportunities.

Over the next few years, they started to appear. He and Kid Moore became friends with Sloan and Rice, who also were newcomers and established cattlemen. Reed started work in slaughtering and meat preparation. He spent a good deal of time at the Pierce City Hotel, and not only because the accommodations suited him: The proprietors did as well.

The place was run by Mary Warren, whose husband, Aaron, was sickly and, when he was well, was often out of town on business. Reed and Mrs. Warren were widely assumed to have had an affair, a turn of discussion that doubtless affected what people in town believed, or were willing to believe, about Bill Reed.

When he was released from St. Joseph's, he returned to the City Hotel. Several months after he had mostly recovered from his injuries in the summer of 1908, tended to by Mary Warren, Reed was finally put on trial. He was bailed out of jail by Mary Warren. At first the charges were attempted murder, for all the shots he had fired on his way to escape. Those charges were dropped. Dan Carr survived the four bullets Reed had fired, but eventually Carr was charged with murder. Two young girls, who had been headed home and were off in the distance when the shooting happened, testified that Carr had opened fire first and that Reed was acting in self-defense. The cattle rustling charges remained, and those alone would be serious enough to put Reed away for years.

Once again, however, he was fortunate. A group of Nez Perce Indians attended the proceedings and said that the previous summer they had bought several cows from the Carrs and sold them to Reed for butchering. They weren't sure about the white and red cow in question, the one whose branded hide had been found in the slaughterhouse, but thought it was likely one of theirs.

Reed was acquitted. Just after the trial, Reed would later say, the prosecutor described him as a "dead shot." That became the name that stuck. Deadshot Reed is how he became known to several generations of Idahoans living in or visiting the backcountry, one of those figures the locals never tired of talking about.

Reed stayed in the Pierce area for another year, working cattle with Sloan and building some financial reserve. Then, in July of 1909, Reed took off for Spokane to elope—not with Mary Warren, but rather with her daughter, Bessie. The official records note her age at eighteen, but other accounts list her as young as thirteen. After a quick return trip to Pierce, they took off for British Columbia, then for Dallas, Oregon, but neither suited.

Reed finally found his homestead back in Idaho, more than a hundred miles south of the Pierce area, well east of McCall on the Salmon River's south fork, some miles outside of a remote settlement called Knox. After the couple's arrival there in 1914, they stayed for the rest of their lives. They raised fourteen children, all but two surviving infancy, and a small herd of cattle; did a little farming; worked a mining claim for a time; and generally lived mainly a subsistence life.

Deadshot Reed may have been deep in the backcountry, but he had neighbors. The nearest, perhaps a half-mile away, was a German immigrant named George Krassel. He was fiercely proud of his old country, and throughout the World War I period he would loudly proclaim its virtues, irritating Reed no end. The two became increasingly annoyed with each other.

One day in June 1919, as the arguments had gotten ever hotter, Krassel showed up on Reed's property. Reed, recovering from a flu that had kept him indoors, was walking around behind the house at the time. As Bessie Reed, inside the house, looked out into the front yard, she thought she saw Krassel carrying a rifle. She grabbed a pistol and handed it to one of the children, who gave it to her father with a message about who was in front. Armed with gun and information, Reed slipped around the side of the house to confront Krassel, who was still on his horse.

As Reed told it, Krassel pulled up his rifle and fired at Reed, but missed. Within a second Reed pulled the pistol from his waistband, fired, and shot Krassel through the heart. The German collapsed on the ground.

An inquiry concluded that Reed had shot him in self-defense and the matter went to rest.

Reed stayed at the ranch on the south fork until the mid-fifties, when he and Bessie moved to a small farm near the town of Sweet. He died there in 1958.

Serial Wife

When Lyda Lewis and Ed Meyer married in September 1920, the nuptials must have struck their neighbors as the cap of a happy story, a reversal of several bad episodes in their lives. And now here they were at the Twin Falls Hospital, only a month later, facing an emergency.

Meyer was the manager of the Blue Lakes Ranch, having worked many years for the patriarch of Twin Falls, Ira Perrine. But it had not been an easy time; the ranch life was wearying, and now he had the chance to settle down.

Lyda Lewis, after growing up in the shadow of the Perrine spread, had married at a young age, only to become a widow just three years later. And then a second marriage—widowed. And a third—widowed. And now her fourth husband was desperately ill. And she was only twenty-eight. But hardly anyone who saw her, hardly anyone male at least, thought about any of that when she came by. She was a striking beauty, her red hair, perfect figure, and pretty face bringing her instant attention wherever she went.

Ed Meyer could only groan in pain because his insides seemed to be on fire.

Doctors had not been able to reach a diagnosis. Ferocious strains of the flu were still sweeping around the country—the disease was said to have carried off one of Lyda's previous husbands—and this latest illness could be that. They asked what he had been eating. For a time, they settled on inadvertent food poisoning, from the sardines and milk he'd been consuming.

They kept him at the hospital under observation, and the days dragged on. Grasping for anything that might work, the doctors tried a battery of tests. None of them seemed to do much good. For a time, Meyer was only hanging on.

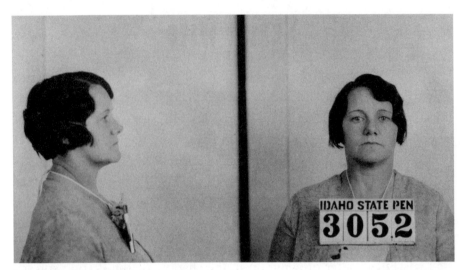

Mugshot of Lyda Lewis
Courtesy Idaho State Historical Society

Then, after six days, Ed Meyer seemed to turn a corner. His fever went down, he breathed easier, and the pain faded. The doctors still weren't sure what was wrong with him, but his stay at the hospital seemed to be helping.

Lyda visited him regularly. The day after he seemed to be on the mend, she approached one of the nurses with a request. The two of them were still newlyweds, she said, and they'd had hardly any time together. She wasn't sure how much longer he'd be cooped up in this hospital and Lyda wanted some time alone with her husband. She'd brought a picnic basket with the fixings for lunch and was hoping for a little private time. The staff was sympathetic. There was not much bureaucracy; the hospital at Twin Falls had opened its doors only two years before. Things were still informal.

Lyda happily took her picnic basket into the room where her husband, still weak from fighting his way back to health, was waiting. They were in there for several hours. Nurses walking past heard their conversation into the mid-afternoon.

Then Lyda threw the door open, panic on her face once again. Something was wrong! Ed was sick again and doubled over with horrific pain, stumbling and falling.

The doctors went to work, trying rapid-speed some of their earlier treatments. Nothing worked.

Early that evening, he died.

They were stunned, puzzled. He had seemed to be doing so well.

They might have been less puzzled if, during the admissions process, Lyda had been required to make a full statement about the couple's insurance policies. They might have found useful a notation that, only a couple of weeks before, she had taken out an insurance policy on Meyer's life, which was now set to pay out to her in the amount of $12,000.

If it is true that children learn about domestic life, and as adults fashion their own, after their childhood family experiences, you have to wonder what it was that Lyda Trueblood could have learned from her father. She might have learned from him the concept of the easy opportunity, and how quickly it can slip away. She might have learned how a lifetime of backbreaking work could only lead to a bare, drab, unsatisfying life.

Certainly she came away with a craving for the fast buck and a taste for high life. But she failed her final exam: All her efforts, all her schemes, all her killings, yielded in the end a sad and dreary life shrouded in obscurity.

But once, she was an international femme fatale—and Idaho's most notorious serial killer.

Lyda was born in 1892 in Keytesville, Missouri, a farming community no bigger today than it was then, now a little more than an hour's drive from Kansas City but then out of reach for ordinary farmers. The 1890s were a desperate period for farmers nationally, a time of populist political unrest, and almost all badly wanted to improve their prospects.

William Trueblood was in that frame of mind when, on a visit to town, he spotted a poster advertising spectacular opportunities in

Idaho. Federal water had just become available in the south-central part of the state, and the whole region was considered almost magical, even being called the Magic Valley.

In late 1906, the Truebloods—William, his wife, a son, and two daughters—packed up and headed west, across the empty deserts, over mountains and streams, much as the Oregon Trail pioneers had decades before. When they arrived, William Trueblood promptly bought a tract of land.

The big profits, made by people like irrigation planner Ira Perrine, were coming from the lands near the Snake River. Trueblood's land was well south of that, watered by the Salmon Falls Dam, but not watered well. As his daughter Lyda, now fourteen, watched him struggle to survive, doing no better in Idaho than he had in Missouri, she picked up on some life lessons.

Brightly red-haired and with a good figure, Lyda attracted plenty of male attention, and she quickly concluded it was the big advantage she had in escaping her father's life. She graduated from Twin Falls High School in 1910, and by then she had her pick of suitors.

Robert Dooley was a young man with family tendrils both in the Magic Valley and in Missouri, and by a few degrees more prosperous than the Truebloods. He had known Lyda back in Missouri, and now offered to take her there. She accepted. They were married in March 1912 in Twin Falls, and then drove back east to Keytesville, where Dooley took over part of the family property. Those two years were not as prosperous as hoped, so they returned to Twin Falls with Dooley's brother Ed and a daughter named Laura Marie in tow, and bought a small farm.

The young family had just started to develop that farm when their neighbors were surprised to hear that Ed Dooley had died of ptomaine poisoning. They were even more surprised to hear, a few months later, in late 1915, that Robert Dooley, too, had died, apparently of the typhoid epidemic that was sweeping the country.

The deaths were investigated, but only lightly. Accidental poisonings sometimes happened on farms, and epidemics were rampant. Only later, after extensive checks and research, would authorities learn that a life insurance policy had been taken out on Ed Dooley, with the payoff of $2,500 going to Robert and Lyda, and that another policy, on Robert, had been taken out too, for $5,000, with Lyda as the beneficiary. The insurance companies paid, and did not think much of it.

Lyda spent some time on the small farm but more often was seen in town, at first the demure widow but soon catching appreciative attention again. Stopping at a cafe in Twin Falls, she fell into a conversation with its owner, Billy McHaffie, and then another, and before long he asked her to marry him. They were married in May 1917, and seemed to people in town to be a happy couple.

All seemed well for a year and more. McHaffie prospered with his cafe and other properties he owned outside of town. Then in the fall of 1918, as headlines around the country warned of a fast-spreading influenza epidemic, Billy McHaffie abruptly fell ill. The speed and the depth of his illness shocked his friends and customers; he had always been a robust, healthy man.

And then the daughter, Laura Marie, died too, evidently of the same disease. To the doctors, both deaths looked like cases of the feared influenza, and they certified them as such.

And then, days after McHaffie's funeral, Lyda Trueblood Dooley McHaffie sold all her property and vanished from Twin Falls.

Only one man knew where she went. One day before Bill McHaffie's death, a farm machinery salesman named Harlan Lewis had come to their door, trying to make a sale. McHaffie noted that Lyda seemed struck by him, and neighbors reported that the couple started arguing a lot more from that point on. When McHaffie died, Lyda split from Twin Falls, apparently not with Lewis but with plans to meet him. They married in Denver, in March 1919.

The happy couple drove north to Lewis's business headquarters at

Billings, Montana. But the new marriage did not last long. In July, just three months after the wedding, Harlan Lewis was dead at Billings. Lyda Trueblood Dooley McHaffie Lewis stayed around long enough to collect on the $10,000 life insurance policy—double most of the previous ones—she had just taken out on Lewis's life. As soon as she cashed out his estate, she vanished again.

So far she had managed to run under the radar of law enforcement, and had she moved on to a new community, she might have extended her streak much longer. But instead she returned to Twin Falls, apparently early in 1920.

There she soon began to socialize with Ed Meyer, a large, powerfully built man who was manager of the Blue Lakes Ranch for businessman Ira Perrine, one of the founders and pillars of Twin Falls.

A few days after Ed Meyer died, Lyda tried to collect on the $12,000 life insurance policy. The company rejected the payout. For all her experience around insurance policies, Lyda had made a mistake with this one because an initial payment had been late. Furious, but determined not to hang around, she disappeared again.

It was this second abrupt disappearance from Twin Falls that caught local attention. The Perrine family applied pressure to get to the bottom of this odd sequence of events. The sheriff needed no pressure to go after the case, since he was an old friend of Meyer's. He assigned Deputy Sheriff Virgil Ormsby to look into it and to find Lyda and clear up the nagging suspicion that something wasn't right.

Ormsby's investigation would take on almost epic dimensions.

Starting with the suspicion of murder, he thoroughly explored the old McHaffie house, now under new ownership. The new owners drew his attention to something unusual in the basement, which had been left over from the McHaffie tenancy: a huge stack of flypaper supplies. Ormsby put the pieces together: Lyda had boiled the flypaper, extracting the arsenic from it, and then poisoned the food of her husbands, and presumably her daughter as well. Arsenic poisoning could be hard to detect if law officials weren't looking for it.

Ormsby began to look for it. He started exhuming bodies, and found trace amounts of arsenic in Myers's and McHaffie's bodies. He developed a strong circumstantial case, with but one problem: Lyda Trueblood Dooley McHaffie Lewis Meyer was nowhere to be found.

She had wandered down to California, working jobs and conserving her money, and finally seizing on Vincent Paul Southard, then the chief petty officer on the USS Monterey. At this point, Lyda was describing herself as a nurse, though she never tried to work as one. Southard fell hard, and within weeks the two were married in Los Angeles, on November 1920. Southard was transferred to Pearl Harbor and Lyda followed him there.

Following one thin lead after another, Ormsby figured that Lyda had moved to the coast. With the help of California law enforcement, he tracked her from one city to another, at one point south of the border into Tijuana, and finally back to the Los Angeles area. There he discovered she had just left for Hawaii, where Chief Petty Office Southard had been transferred.

Hoping to block another poisoning, Ormsby called law enforcement at Honolulu. They followed both of Ormsby's instructions: to arrest Lyda and to check around to see if any life insurance policy had been taken out on her new husband, with Lyda the beneficiary. One had been, and it consequently was canceled.

Brought back to Twin Falls to stand trial, Lyda Southard became an international celebrity, tracked by news photographers on her trip back to Idaho and during the trial. Her latest husband, Southard, accompanied her, not believing that his new bride could be a killer. Lyda generally seemed to enjoy the attention, and she gave interviews. But one profile of her, in the *San Francisco Call and Post*, seemed to shake her: "Her face is that of a weak woman capable of committing the crimes of which she is accused, yet unconscious of her guilt."

Lyda Trueblood Dooley McHaffie Lewis Meyer Southard was jailed and, in September 1921, tried in the same courthouse where she'd signed three marriage licenses. But despite the hoopla, her trial was a somber affair, detailed and protracted. Prosecutors pulled out bottles of liver and spleen—the exhibits were called "grisly." Lasting seven weeks, it was the longest criminal trial in Idaho up to then.

She was convicted of second-degree murder; speculation ran that jurors blanched at the idea of hanging a woman. But they had no doubt about her guilt, and after watching the trial neither did Paul Southard, who finally filed for divorce.

Prisoner 3052 was sentenced to life imprisonment. Walking around the old rock penitentiary, she developed a schedule of her own, ironically a more domestic one: Her hours were spent in sewing, gardening, and listening to music on an old Victrola. She was a little shy of thirty years old.

As the years passed, the quiet and demure prisoner was gradually given more leeway at the prison. Rumors of relationships with staff at the prison were of questionable authenticity, but in 1931, as she approached a decade behind bars, she definitely established a romantic relationship with an inmate named David Minton.

In the middle of the night in May 1931, two weeks after Minton was released from prison, Lyda broke through the bars on her window and climbed down a hand-fashioned rope, and then down the trellises of the roses she had so carefully tended. Minton met her outside and they drove off in his car.

A frantic search ensued for months but it came up empty. Police finally caught Minton in Denver, but Lyda wasn't with him; he maintained that they'd split up weeks before and he didn't know where she was. For several weeks he stuck to that story. But after he was rearrested (for helping her escape) and returned to Idaho, he admitted he did have a clue.

Authorities were closing in on Lyda when she got married again, in Denver to Harry Whitlock. Just before detectives arrived at their house, she split after getting some travel money from Whitlock. Calling herself Fern at this point, she had hooked up with him initially by doing housekeeping work. She had suggested a $20,000 life insurance policy on him, but it hadn't been purchased by the time she left.

Lyda was finally picked up in Kansas, and the Whitlock marriage was annulled. She was returned to Boise fifteen months after her escape.

Lyda stayed in prison most of the next decade, but then public attitudes toward longtime prisoners began to change. In October 1941 she was released to the home of her sister, Blanche Quigley, and Blanche's husband, John, at Nyssa, Oregon. She lived a quiet life there and was fully pardoned on October 1943. For a couple of years she stayed there, but then wanderlust hit. She returned to the family farm at Twin Falls, but her relatives and other townspeople didn't welcome her presence.

After some months she moved on to Provo, Utah, where she wasn't known, and there scraped together enough money to buy a small secondhand shop. She met a man named Hal Shaw and married him. Then Shaw's children found out about Lyda's past, and one day Shaw vanished from Lyda's sight. She later moved to Salt Lake City and worked as a housekeeper and waitress. She died in February 1958, apparently of a heart attack.

She was buried in Utah, under the name of Lyda Shaw.

Suggested Reading

Outlaws in the American West have been a popular subject ever since they were around doing their dirty deeds, or in some cases being wrongly accused of them. Most libraries of even modest size will include a number of volumes about crime on the frontier.

One of the most enjoyable, even half a century since its publication, is the *Pictorial history of the Wild West: A true account of the bad men, desperadoes, rustlers, and outlaws of the old West—and the men who fought them to establish law and order,* by James David Horan (Crown, 1954).

A more recent and highly dramatic overview of some of the bad men of the West is *Draw: The Greatest Gunfights of the American West,* by James Reasoner (Berkley Publishing, 2003).

For general local storytelling about Idaho history, one book stands preeminent: *Idaho for the Curious,* by Cort Conley (Backeddy Books, 1982). Its 704 pages, organized as a highway travelogue, are a wealth of background about the places of Idaho, including many of the amusing, chastening, or sometimes simply odd stories in its past. *Idaho for the Curious* makes references to a number of the crimes and criminals in this book.

Probably the finest single piece of sustained historical writing about Idaho is *Big Trouble,* by J. Anthony Lukas (Simon & Schuster, 1997). Ostensibly about the Big Bill Haywood trial of 1906 (mentioned briefly in this book, in the chapter about Harry Orchard), it is actually about much more—about the whole American scene of that era. It contains a remarkably detailed and precise account of Boise in the new twentieth century, a fascinating picture that rewards rereading. Besides touching on the Orchard case, Lukas brings in a great deal of other material, including the Levy murder case in Boise.

Finally, I'd be remiss not to mention another book, an overview of Idaho history you might well enjoy if you enjoyed this book: *It*

Happened in Idaho, published by The Globe Pequot Press and written by the author of this present volume.

A few specific notes about some of the incidents recounted in this book:

- The Magruder murders have entered into the category of basic Idaho lore, moderately well known among historians even if a little obscure yet to the general public. The most thorough accounting of the incident, and the most enjoyable read, is *This Bloody Deed*. Author Ladd Hamilton, a longtime editor at the daily newspaper at Lewiston, devoted years pulling together the details of the case and carefully examined court records and other documents unavailable to many earlier researchers. The book's usefulness is limited only by Hamilton's "novelizing" the story in some places.

  All of the references are useful, however, and balance competing points of view when accounts differ, as they do in several instances. Julia Welch in *The Magruder Murders*, for example, concluded that Henry Plummer was not involved with the Magruder murders, while Hamilton thought otherwise.

- The Patterson-Pinkham feud generated no books or magazine articles, but veteran Idaho historian Arthur Hart did devote a chapter of his Idaho City history, *Basin of Gold: Life in Boise Basin, 1862–1890*, to the feud, and especially its aftermath. Several lengthy recollections of the events have also survived. Clyde L. Johnson's report, "Ferd Patterson," piecing together many of the details, dates from the 1950s.

- The primary references on the Levy case come from the extensive newspaper coverage in the *Idaho Statesman* in 1901, although the coverage has to be dissected carefully; much of the prose was purple, and so was some of the reporting.

The case is also referenced, substantially, in an extensive Boise State University thesis study of prostitution in Boise, which provides significant useful guidance. It also turns up in a more limited but still useful way in Lukas's *Big Trouble*.

- Of all the figures in this book, none has been scrutinized more thoroughly by historians than Harry Orchard, the assassin of a governor and for a brief time, a century ago, a name known internationally.

David Grover's *Debaters and Dynamiters* for some years stood as the leading account of the Orchard case and its aftermath, and it remains the most thorough account of the Haywood trial itself. More recently, the massive and magisterial *Big Trouble*, by J. Anthony Lukas, which focused on the Steunenberg assassination and its aftermath, has emerged as what looks like the last word on the larger-picture subject. Although not focusing on Orchard personally, it included a detailed and (as with everything else in the book) exhaustively researched section about him. *Big Trouble* and its sources have been a key source for this chapter.

Many of the confessions in this chapter, however, are primarily based not on *Big Trouble, Debaters and Dynamiters,* or the widely published 1907 Orchard autobiography *The Confessions and Autobiography of Harry Orchard,* but on a more recent development. In the spring of 2006 the estate of Governor Frank Gooding delivered to the Idaho Historical Society a new version of Orchard's confessions—actually, the first version of his confessions, before Orchard, attorneys, and others began gently massaging them. Even the original margin notes are visible. This chapter is based primarily on this newly discovered confession; there is some thought among Idaho historians that the newly discovered version may be a little closer to Orchard's actual story but, as noted in the chapter, it should not be taken as indisputable truth. A photocopy of it is available for review in the special documents room of the Idaho Historical Society.

- We should note a serious difficulty in telling the story of Deadshot Reed: The accounts of his life vary so sharply that certainty is elusive. Most of what is available can be found in two short book-length accounts, which at times seem almost to be describing two different men. One is a near memoir, the "as-told-to" account *Rewards of Rage*, by Art Colson. It has the advantage of emerging, to a degree at least, from the mouth of the horse, since Colson was an acquaintance of Reed's from the thirties until his death in 1958. Reed and some of his family members apparently were the main sources for the book. The problem is the flip side of that: Reed's own memory of some long-ago events may have been faulty, and—in the manner of more than one figure of the old West—in places he may have let a good story trump the facts. Beyond that, Reed had been dead nearly forty years by the time the book was published, allowing for more discrepancies. Still, it can't be disregarded: It is the closest we have to Reed's own perspective.

  For Better or For Worse, written six years later (and evidently partly in response to Colson's book) by Kathy Hill, is a more conventional biography lacking some of the color of *Rewards of Rage* but with broader research through the paper record and more interviews.

  The chapter in this book relies more on the Hill treatment than on Colson, but incorporates some of the references in each.

  There are also indirect personal accounts. The author's wife talked with one of Reed's sons, Pat, on a number of occasions in the 1970s, and Deadshot Reed stories have circulated regularly over the years in the central Idaho backcountry.

- Finally, the story of the serial-killing wife has been irresistible for a number of writers. The most extensive treatment (novelized but largely factual) is in William Anderson's *Lady Bluebeard*. (Anderson is best known for his Vietnam book *BAT-21*, which was made into a motion picture.) In his research Anderson collected a number of original source materials for his book, and those original materials are still located in his collection at the Albertson Library at Boise State University, Boise. The author extends thanks to the family for permission to examine and quote from those materials.

References

The Magruder Incident

Hamilton, Ladd. *This Bloody Deed: The Magruder Incident.* Pullman, WA: Washington State University Press, 1994.

Langford, Nathaniel. *Vigilante Days and Ways.* Helena, MT: Farcountry Press, 1995.

Limbaugh, Ronald. "The Year Without a Code," *Idaho Yesterdays,* Spring 1981, p. 13.

Loeffler, Fred. *The Avenging Innkeeper: Magruder Party Murder.* Melba, ID: Yates Publishing, 1972.

Welch, Julia Conway. *The Magruder Murders: Coping with violence on the western frontier.* Helena, MT: Falcon Press, 1991.

The Opportunist

Limbaugh, Ronald H. *Rocky Mountain Carpetbaggers.* Moscow, ID: University Press of Idaho, 1977.

McConnell, William. *Early History of Idaho.* Caldwell, ID: Caxton Printers, 1913.

McFadden, Thomas G. "We'll All Wear Diamonds," *Idaho Yesterdays,* Summer 1966, pp. 2–7.

A Civil War Reenactment

Davis, Hester. Personal recollection, dated "1866 or 1867," in files of Idaho Historical Society, "Crime and Criminal" folder.

Hart, Arthur. *Basin of Gold: Life in Boise Basin, 1862–1890.* Idaho City, ID: Idaho City Historical Foundation, 1986.

Idaho Statesman. "Early Idaho Feud Nearly Started Territorial Civil War," February 27, 1930.

Johnson, Clyde L. "Ferd Patterson," unpublished and undated report in the files of Idaho Historical Society, "Crime and Criminal" folder.

Justice Overtaken

Idaho Sheriffs Association. "History of Idaho sheriff's offices," 1998.

Idaho Statesman, September 24, 1950.

Langford, Nathaniel. *Vigilante Days and Ways.* Helena, MT: Farcountry Press, 1995.

Lindstron, Joyce, including essays by William McConnell, James Reynolds, and others. "Idaho Vigilantes." Boise, ID: Idaho Research Foundation, 1984.

McConnell, William. *Early History of Idaho.* Caldwell, ID: Caxton Printers, 1913.

The Storyteller

Adams, Mildretta. *Historic Silver City.* Nampa, ID: Schwartz Printing Co., 1969.

d'Easum, Dick. *Sawtooth Tales.* Caldwell, ID: Caxton Printers, 1977.

Hanley, Mike, with Ellis Lucia. *Owyhee Trails.* Caldwell, ID: Caxton Printers, 1975.

Welch, Julia Conway. *Gold Town to Ghost Town.* Moscow, ID: University of Idaho Press, 1982.

Counterfeit

Conley, Cort. *Idaho for the Curious.* Cambridge, ID: Backeddy Books, 1982.

Elsensohn, Sister M. Alfreda. *Pioneer Days in Idaho County.* Caldwell, ID: Caxton Press, 1951.

Idaho County Free Press. "Counterfeiting case verdict," June 4, 1897.

Moscow Mirror articles. May 1897.

Diamondfield Jack

Conley, Cort. *Idaho for the Curious.* Cambridge, ID: Backeddy Books, 1982.

Grover, Davis. *Diamondfield Jack: A Study in Frontier Justice.* Norman: University of Oklahoma Press, 1986.

Idaho State Historical Society. "Jackson Lee Davis AKA Diamondfield Jack, Inmate #820," undated article on Web site of the Idaho State Historical Society, www.idahohistory.net/OldPenDiamondfield.pdf, referenced August 10, 2006.

The Montpelier Job

Lyon, Suzanne. *Bandit Invincible: Butch Cassidy, a Western Story.* New York: Five Star, 2000.

Patterson, Richard M. *Butch Cassidy, a Biography.* Lincoln: University of Nebraska Press, 1998.

Pointer, Larry. *In Search of Butch Cassidy.* Norman: University of Oklahoma Press, 1977.

Stapilus, Randy. *It Happened in Idaho.* Guilford, CT: The Globe Pequot Press, 2001.

In Levy's Alley

Idaho Statesman articles, principally October 6, 7, 8, 21, and 22, 1901.

Lukas, J. Anthony. *Big Trouble.* New York: Simon & Schuster, 1997.

Russell, Jo Anne. *A Necessary Evil: Prostitution, Patriarchs and Profits in Boise City, 1863–1915.* Thesis, Boise, ID: Boise State University, 1991.

The Assassin

Grover, David. *Debaters and Dynamiters: The Story of the Haywood Trial.* Corvallis: Oregon State University Press, 1964.

Johnson, Claudius. *Borah of Idaho.* New York: Longmans, Green & Co., 1936.

Lukas, J. Anthony. *Big Trouble.* New York: Simon & Schuster, 1997.

Orchard, Harry. *The Confessions and Autobiography of Harry Orchard.* New York: McClure Company, 1907.

————. Original transcript of interview. January, 1906.

Deadshot

Clearwater Historical Museum. "Clearwater County," undated article on the Web at http://home.valint.net/chmuseum/CCHistory.htm, accessed October 18, 2006.

Colson, Art. *Rewards of Rage.* Middleton, ID: CHJ Publishing, 1997.

Hill, Kathy. *For Better or For Worse.* McCall, ID: Big Mallard Books, 2003.

Serial Wife

Anderson, William C. *Lady Bluebeard: The True Story of Love and Marriage, Death and Flypaper.* Boulder, CO: Fred Pruett Books, 1994.

Arentz, Bob. *Murder in Idaho: A compilation of famous Idaho crimes.* Idaho State Historical Society files, 1946.

Argosy magazine. "Lady Bluebeard," April 1957.

Rhodenbaugh, Edward F. *Toxicological Investigation in the case of William Gordon McHaffie, deceased, of Twin Falls, Idaho.* Submitted September 8, 1921. Copies available in the Anderson collection at the Albertson Library at Boise State University, Boise, ID, and elsewhere.

About the Author

Randy Stapilus is an author, blogger, newsletter publisher, and former newspaper reporter and editor. He also wrote *It Happened in Idaho,* published by The Globe Pequot Press. A longtime Idaho resident, he now lives in Carlton, Oregon, with his wife, Linda, a cat, and a varying number of dogs.